FIVE POINTS LEARNING

how to solve

SHSAT
SCRAMBLED
PARAGRAPHS

VOLUME 2

STUDY GUIDE FOR THE NEW YORK CITY
SPECIALIZED HIGH SCHOOL ADMISSIONS TEST

STUYVESANT
BRONX SCIENCE
BROOKLYN TECH
STATEN ISLAND TECH

BROOKLYN LATIN
CITY COLLEGE
LEHMAN COLLEGE
YORK COLLEGE

· EXPERT STRATEGIES TO GIVE YOU THE EDGE ON THE TEST
· 100 SCRAMBLED PARAGRAPHS WITH EXPLANATIONS

HOW TO SOLVE

SHSAT

SCRAMBLED PARAGRAPHS
VOLUME 2
2013

HOW TO SOLVE
SHSAT
SCRAMBLED PARAGRAPHS
VOLUME 2
2013

By the Staff of Five Points Learning Test Prep and Admissions

 FIVE POINTS LEARNING

New York

© 2013 by Five Points Learning, Inc.
Published by Five Points Publishing, a division of Five Points Learning, Inc.
1270 Broadway, Suite 1104
New York, NY 10001
E-mail: publisher@fivepointslearning.com

ISBN-10:0985966017
ISBN-13:978-0-9859660-1-0

Publisher, Edward Song
Senior Editor, Noah Redfield
Editor, Justine Bottles
Editor, Brian Kirchner

Printed in the United States of America
10 9 8 7 6 5 4 3 2 1
July 2013

Five Points Publishing books are available at special quantity discounts. For
more information or to purchase books, please call our special sales department
at (212) 257 - 2264.

TABLE OF CONTENTS

—— INTRODUCTION: WELCOME BACK!

Thank you for purchasing the second volume of our How to Solve SHSAT Scrambled Paragraphs workbook. We received such a positive and strong reaction to our first volume of How to Solve SHSAT Scrambled Paragraphs that we decided to create another book based on the feedback we received.

If you play a musical instrument or participate in a sport, then you understand the value of practice. While 100 Scrambled Paragraphs is certainly helpful, there isn't any harm in another hundred practice problems to hone your skills on the most elusive part of the SHSAT.

So if you have the first volume and have worked through all the paragraphs, great! Here are some more. By the time you take the SHSAT, you will be the best Scrambled Paragraphs taker you can be!

Once again, we've divided the paragraphs up into 20 practice tests. After each test, you can check your answers and study the provided explanations, so you can better get a sense of how the Department of Education thinks when they put the tests together. We've also included a study guide before the tests just in case you need to refresh yourself on the basic strategies.

Any questions? Then let's get started, shall we?

WHAT ARE SCRAMBLED PARAGRAPHS?

The SHSAT Verbal section begins with 5 Scrambled Paragraphs worth two points apiece. Each paragraph begins with a topic sentence followed by five supporting sentences that have been scrambled into the wrong order. All five sentences must be rearranged correctly in order to receive full credit.

HOW DO THEY WORK?

The five supporting sentences follow the topic sentence with the letters Q, R, S, T, and U. To the left of each letter is a line. Observe:

PARAGRAPH 1

Although quicksand has a frightening reputation, it is impossible to sink below one's waist.

_____ **Q.** It is best to use a walking stick to feel for this soft mixture before you find yourself trapped.

_____ **R.** This is because quicksand is formed from a mixture of sand, clay, and water, all of which combined is less dense than the human body.

_____ **S.** However, if you do find yourself trapped in quicksand, remain calm and do not try to fight your way out.

_____ **T.** Instead, lie back and spread your body across the surface in order to float.

_____ **U.** Once you are floating, swim slowly until you reach solid ground.

Use these lines to order the sentences from 1 to 5. That way, you can transfer the correct order to the answer grid more easily.

Speaking of which, let's take a look at a sample answer grid:

Paragraph 1					
The second sentence is	Q	**R**	S	T	U
The third sentence is	Q	R	**S**	T	U
The fourth sentence is	Q	R	S	**T**	U
The fifth sentence is	Q	R	S	T	**U**
The sixth sentence is	**Q**	R	S	T	U

Bubbling in the answers correctly is going to be a real pain unless you rank the sentences beforehand. ***Don't rely on your memory!***

FINDING THE RIGHT ORDER: THE SIGNS

Let's say you're taking a cross-country trip from New York to Los Angeles. How do you know if you're going in the right direction? You follow the signs. What happens if you go to the mall and you're having trouble finding your favorite food court? You follow the signs. So how do you determine the right order for these Scrambled Paragraphs? **You follow the signs.**

There are five signs that you need to look for in every paragraph.

1. Transitions

Transitions indicate whether the sentence agrees with the rest of the paragraph or if it's changing gears instead.

Take another look at that quicksand paragraph and see if you can identify any transition words:

PARAGRAPH 1

Although quicksand has a frightening reputation, it is impossible to sink below one's waist.

_____ **Q.** It is best to use a walking stick to feel for this soft mixture before you find yourself trapped.

_____ **R.** This is because quicksand is formed from a mixture of sand, clay, and water, all of which combined is less dense than the human body.

_____ **S.** However, if you do find yourself trapped in quicksand, remain calm and do not try to fight your way out.

_____ **T.** Instead, lie back and spread your body across the surface in order to float.

_____ **U.** Once you are floating, swim slowly until you reach solid ground.

You should have spotted the words **although**, **however**, and **instead**. The topic sentence explains that **although** quicksand has a frightening reputation, it is impossible to sink to the bottom of a quicksand pit. However, if you are trapped in quicksand, don't try to fight your way out (S). Instead, spread your body out slowly (T).

Upon closer examination, "instead" in T must be referring back to S as it responds to the mistake of fighting quicksand with instructions on how best to handle the problem.

We now know for sure that S and T will be paired together in that order. We don't know where the pairing will fall in the paragraph yet, but we are one step closer to confirming the correct order of the five sentences. And that's based on one sign alone! Now, let's see how the other sentences will match up.

2. Repetition, Repetition, Repetition

If you can identify the repetition of names, places, actions, or objects, you may be able to further lock down the right order. Again: If you can identify the repetition of names, places, actions, or objects, you may be able to further lock down the right order. Once more with feeling: ***If you can identify the repetition of names, places, actions, or objects, you may be able to further lock down the right order.***

Let's go back to the wonderful world of quicksand and look for any repeating words.

PARAGRAPH 1

Although quicksand has a frightening reputation, it is impossible to sink below one's waist.

_____ **Q.**   It is best to use a walking stick to feel for this soft mixture before you find yourself trapped.

_____ **R.**   This is because quicksand is formed from a mixture of sand, clay, and water, all of which combined is less dense than the human body.

_____ **S.**   However, if you do find yourself trapped in quicksand, remain calm and do not try to fight your way out.

_____ **T.**   Instead, lie back and spread your body across the surface in order to float.

_____ **U.**   Once you are floating, swim slowly until you reach solid ground.

For example, do you notice the words "float" and "floating" in sentences T and U, respectively? Take a look at the sentences in more detail. Which had to come first?

T instructs you to float while U explains what to do once you're floating, so logically, T comes before U. And we already know that S is before T let's put the letters together: STU.

Another repeating word is "mixture," found in Q and R. Let's scrutinize these sentences and find out which one has to come first.

That's right: R must come before Q as it explains how the mixture works while Q merely refers to the mixture. Now, let's put these letters together: RQ.

Where is RQ most likely to fall: Before or after STU?

It's hard to say for sure. We need another sign.

Pronouns

Go back to R. To what is "this" referring? It calls back to the fact that one cannot sink below the waist in quicksand, which we learned in the topic sentence. Therefore, R has to be as close to the topic sentence as possible, meaning that the RQ pairing must be at the beginning.

Thanks to these three signs, we have the complete order: RQSTU. And that's your first Scrambled Paragraph complete. Congratuwelldone![1]

You already know that pronouns stand in for nouns. Use this to your advantage!

By way of another example, Q contains the phrase, "this soft mixture." The pronoun "this" indicates that some sentence came before, which was R because of the repetition sign. You will find many more paragraphs containing a plethora of pronouns to serve your unscrambling needs.

---

1   The authors acknowledge that "congratuwelldone" is not a real word. **But** it should be.

But enough about quicksand, let's talk about something a little more appetizing:

PARAGRAPH 2

The origins of pizza can be found in historical records dating all the way back to 1000 A.D.

_5_ Q. Although American pizzerias already existed, this heightened demand helped make the Italian dish one of the most popular foods in the country.

_3_ R. These pizzas were sold in Naples' market stalls, and were baked in ovens fueled by volcanic rock from nearby Mount Vesuvius.

_2_ S. But the first pizzas resembling those we eat today appeared years later in Naples.

_1_ T. These writings refer to a circle of cooked dough with a variety of toppings piled on top.

_4_ U. During WWII, United States servicemen "discovered" pizza in Italy and wanted to see more of it when they returned home.

With a brand new paragraph comes a brand new sign.

Intro Words

Look out for anything that sounds like an introduction. Writers typically don't use intro words to finish off their paragraphs.

If sentence S is talking about *the first pizzas*, it's unlikely that the sentence will appear towards the end.

Say, why don't you try finishing the paragraph yourself? Remember to look for transitions, repetitions, and pronouns as well. You'll find the answers and explanations on page 17.

Let's take a look at one more paragraph:

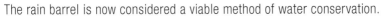

PARAGRAPH 3

The rain barrel is now considered a viable method of water conservation.

_1_ **Q.** This is because water can be gathered during the rainy season and then used during the dry season.

_2_ **R.** While the water collected during the rainy season is not safe for drinking, it is excellent for gardening, landscaping, and cleaning.

_4_ **S.** However, make sure that your barrels are properly secured and covered to keep any insects out.

_3_ **T.** Moreover, rain barrels can store up to 150 gallons of unpurified water, so you won't need to use any drinking water for these activities.

_5_ **U.** On a final note, remember to have your water tested before using it for gardening vegetables. *last*

And with that, here's the fifth and final Scrambled Paragraphs sign.

Conclusion Words

Sometimes, they'll spell it out for you by writing, "in conclusion." Other times, words like, "and so," "finally" or "therefore" will tip you off that the sentence belongs at the end. Either way, keep an eye out for conclusion words. If writers don't use intro words at the end, it's unlikely that they'll insert conclusion words when they're first kicking off their paragraphs.

What's the one phrase in this paragraph that could only appear at the end? That is correct: *On a final note.* This phrase is just one of many examples of conclusion words that you might see on the SHSAT. No matter what happens, sentence U must be involved in the wrap-up.

Now that you have all five signs in your lexicon, care to finish the paragraph? Remember to look up the answers and explanations on page 17.

RECAP

Transitions. Repetition. Pronouns. Intro Words. Conclusion Words.
The signs are always there in plain sight; you just need to look for them.

As you go through the 100 paragraphs, here are some extra pointers:

Basic Advice

- **DO THESE LAST!** Again, you've done Reading Comprehension a billion times in school, so why not stay within your comfort zone and do those first? Save the headache until the end. As the test is not in order of difficulty, you should focus on getting as many raw points as possible in the simpler sections. The *safest* order for the Verbal is Reading, Logical Reasoning, and then Scrambled Paragraphs.
- **WORK SLOWLY!** Speeding through the test will not guarantee a high score; if anything, you're more likely to make one careless mistake after another. The slower you work, the more points you will rack up. ACCURACY OVER SPEED.
- **WRITE EVERYTHING DOWN!** Scrambled Paragraphs are complicated enough without trying to juggle everything mentally. By constantly taking notes, you decrease the chances of becoming confused and messing up the order. GET OUT OF YOUR HEAD; IT'S A BAD NEIGH-BORHOOD.
- **TRUST YOUR INSTINCTS!** Some of these paragraphs will be tougher than others. The signs are your best and only tools, but if you're still having trouble, go with your gut. Don't be afraid to guess.

And Finally...

RELAX! If you wind up in panic mode, you won't be able to think clearly or work effectively. Stay positive, have faith in yourself, and try your best.

Your scrambled paragraphs await. Good luck!

——— ANSWERS & EXPLANATIONS

PARAGRAPH 1 (RQSTU)

The topic sentence debunks the common myth that quicksand sucks its victims underneath the ground. R then explains why it is a myth and describes what components make up quicksand (a mixture of sand, water, and clay). Q links to R with the warning that it is best to use a walking stick to feel for "this soft mixture" before you find yourself stuck in the quicksand. S changes gears with "however" and explains what not to do if you're trapped in quicksand. T then explains how you should position yourself in order to float. U leads with "Once you are floating," and concludes with the victim reaching solid ground.

PARAGRAPH 2 (TSRUQ)

The topic sentence introduces the first records of pizza in 1000 A.D. T elaborates on these historical references. S transitions into the pizzas we eat today and declares Naples the origin city. R must follow as it elaborates on its place in the Naples marketplace. U states that U.S. Servicemen "discovered" pizza while in Italy and wanted more of it back in the United States. Q gives the effect of "this heightened demand," which was to make pizza one of the most popular foods in the country.

PARAGRAPH 3 (QRTSU)

The topic sentence introduces rain barrels as a popular way to conserve water. Q explains why this is a viable method and summarizes how the process works. R states that the water is not safe for drinking but is useful for the other listed activities. T starts with "moreover," a transition that agrees with the previous sentence, and elaborates on why you don't need to use the water for drinking. S changes gears with the word "however" and reminds the reader to make sure the barrels mentioned in T are properly secured. U leads with, "On a final note," which can only be the paragraph's concluding sentence.

Scrambled Paragraphs
Tests 1-20

TEST ONE

PARAGRAPH 1

Many people don't realize that the popular American folk song, "Battle Hymn of the Republic," is taken from a different tune altogether.

___3___ **Q.** A poet named Julia Ward Howe heard a performance of this song and decided to write new lyrics for it.

___5___ **R.** Both versions enjoy popularity to this day and have been recorded and performed by several different artists.

___2___ **S.** Brown led an unsuccessful slave revolt in 1859 that would become one of many causes of the Civil War.

___4___ **T.** Howe's version, which she titled "Battle Hymn of the Republic," was first published in the Atlantic Monthly three years after Brown's actions.

___1___ **U.** "John Brown's Body" was written by Union soldiers at the beginning of the Civil War in honor of John Brown.

U S Q T R

PARAGRAPH 2

Sea snails can be found all throughout the four oceans and have many uses.

___5___ **Q.** For example, hermit crabs seek out their abandoned shells and utilize them for protection.

___1___ **R.** One of their most common uses is that of jewelry.

___2___ **S.** These seashells have been used to make necklaces as far back as prehistoric times

___3___ **T.** Many of the seashells we often find on beaches originally come from sea snails.

___4___ **U.** Even other animals make use of sea snails and their shells.

R S T U Q

PARAGRAPH 3

The Cassowary is one of the largest and most exotic birds in the world.

_3_ **Q.** In addition, more than half of these deaths resulted from contact with oncoming vehicles.

_2_ **R.** In Queensland, Australia, the Southern Cassowary is classified as endangered with approximately a quarter of its original habitat remaining.

_1_ **S.** This flightless bird can be found in the rainforests of New Guinea as well as parts of Australia.

_4_ **T.** Officials have put up road signs throughout Queensland warning drivers, "Speeding has killed Cassowaries."

_5_ **U.** Nevertheless, the Cassowary continues to fight off extinction in the face of vehicles as well as dogs and humans.

S R Q T U ✓

PARAGRAPH 4

If you climb to the top of St. Paul's Cathedral in London, you can take in a view of nearly the entire city.

_1_ **Q.** After the Great Fire of London destroyed the previous St. Paul's in 1666, an architect named Sir Christopher Wren was given the task of rebuilding the cathedral.

_3_ **R.** His most significant change was a dome in the shape of a lantern to sit atop the cathedral that contrasted with the old building's tall steeple.

_5_ **S.** However, the cathedral remains standing despite enduring the horrors of the Blitz in the 1940s.

_4_ **T.** Work on the new St. Paul's was completed in 1711 to a mixed response.

_2_ **U.** Wren's new design adhered to late English baroque architecture and moved away from the Gothic origins of the old St. Paul's.

Q U R T S ✓

PARAGRAPH 5

For twenty years, Long John Nebel was one of the most prominent talk show hosts broadcasting in New York radio.

_2_ **Q.** Despite this, Nebel's unusual program gathered a cult audience that followed him throughout his career.

_5_ **R.** He eventually settled down at WMCA and continued broadcasting until his death.

_3_ **S.** Among the bizarre subjects explored on his program included UFOs, witchcraft, and various conspiracy theories.

_1_ **T.** Nebel first started on WOR with a slot that began at 5:30am, which was the least popular time slot for the station.

_4_ **U.** Nebel left WOR for a better slot on WNBC but left that station after he refused to play rock and roll music on his show.

T Q S U R ✓

ANSWERS & EXPLANATIONS: TEST ONE

Paragraph 1 (USQTR)

The topic sentence establishes that the origins of "Battle Hymn of the Republic" may be unknown to most people. U follows as it explains what the origin specifically is; U introduces John Brown, while S elaborates on who Brown was. Q follows with a performance of the original song, and introduces Julia Ward Howe. T has Howe writing the new lyrics, and R concludes with a statement about the continued popularity of both songs.

Paragraph 2 (RTSUQ)

The topic sentence establishes that sea snails have many uses. R must follow as it introduces one specific use, which is jewelry. T follows because it is the first sentence to mention seashells while informing us that many of them come from sea snails. S comes next because it ties in the reference to jewelry in R with the reference to seashells in T. U changes the subject from humans and jewelry to that of animals, so it has to come fourth. Finally, Q wraps up the paragraph with one example of an animal making use of sea snails.

Paragraph 3 (SRQTU)

The topic sentence introduces the Cassowary by listing two of its attributes. S refers back to the topic sentence directly with the phrase, "this flightless bird," and introduces Australia as one of its habitats. R carries on with a specific Australian city wherein the Cassowary is endangered. Q offers up a specific reason for this problem, while T provides an example of the Queensland authorities attempting to curb the issue. U uses the transition word "nevertheless" to reaffirm the fact that the Cassowary is still fighting off predators as a way of concluding the paragraph.

Paragraph 4 (QURTS)

The topic sentence starts a paragraph about St. Paul's Cathedral in London with a trivial fact. Q is the first sentence as it establishes the subject of the cathedral's construction while introducing the designer, Sir Christopher Wren. U elaborates on Wren's design and how it differed from past designs. R provides a specific example of one of Wren's innovations. T follows with the completion of St. Paul's along with its mixed reception. S concludes with St. Paul's withstanding even in the face of tremendous hardships.

Paragraph 5 (TQSUR)

The topic sentence introduces the broadcaster Long John Nebel. T must follow as it introduces his first major job in radio at WOR and its dreadful time slot. Q comes next with Nebel's "unusual program" reaching a following despite the time slot mention in T. S elaborates on the nature of "his program." U has Nebel leaving WOR for WNBC, while R ends the paragraph with Nebel settling in at WMCA until his death.

———————— TEST TWO

PARAGRAPH 1

The story of the RMS Titanic's construction is almost as interesting as that of the ship's doomed maiden voyage.

_5_ **Q.** Because of the Titanic's tragic sinking in 1912, the struggles of the men who built the ship have largely been forgotten.

_3_ **R.** Over 200 of these men suffered injuries due to unsafe working conditions.

_1_ **S.** Harland & Wolff, a construction company based in Northern Ireland, was tasked with building the ocean liner in 1909.

_4_ **T.** Worse, an additional nine men lost their lives.

_2_ **U.** 15,000 Irish workers labored over the Titanic's construction, often at the risk of their lives.

S U R T Q

PARAGRAPH 2

The Battle of Algiers, directed by Gillo Pontecorvo, depicts the Algerian struggle for independence against the French in the 1950s.

_3_ **Q.** He achieved this by shooting in real locations and using non-actors for the majority of the roles.

_1_ **R.** Specifically, it portrays the guerrilla tactics employed by the oppressed people of Algiers.

_5_ **S.** Today, it is screened and analyzed for film students, sociologists, and military strategists alike.

_2_ **T.** Pontecorvo aimed to show these tactics in as realistic a manner as possible.

_4_ **U.** Upon its release, _The Battle of Algiers_ received widespread critical acclaim but was banned in France for five years.

R T Q U S

PARAGRAPH 3

The World Chess Championship is held every year to determine who the greatest player on Earth is.

1 Q. Founded in 1886, the championship operated under the rules determined by the previous champion for nearly sixty years.

3 R. Many years later, Garry Kasparov broke away from FIDE and created a rival chess competition.

2 S. Then, in 1948, an organization called the FIDE began regulating the rules of the game.

5 T. The rivalry continued until Kasparov lost the title, and in 2006, the classical and official champions played against each other for the first time.

4 U. Kasparov dubbed his new competition, the Classical World Chess Championship.

QSRTU X
QSRUT

PARAGRAPH 4

Although millions of people enjoy watching live comedy shows, the process of putting one together is not as fun as it looks.

2 Q. These scripts need to be approved by the head writer, who will revise and rewrite the sketches until they are perfect.

3 R. Then, the show's producers need to approve the completed sketches before passing them along to the director and cast members.

4 S. Once each sketch has been cast, the actors have only a few days to learn their lines and practice performing before a live studio audience.

1 T. First, a team of comedy writers need to turn in new scripts every week.

5 U. On the night of the show, everyone involved is fully prepared to deliver one hour of comedy sketches to the delight of their audience.

TQRSU

PARAGRAPH 5

In 1642, Rembrandt van Rijn unveiled the most famous of all his paintings, the Night Watch.

3 **Q.** Banning Cocq personally commissioned Rembrandt to do the group portrait and the militia paid him an enormous amount of money to do so.

5 **R.** Over the years, the painting has suffered multiple acts of vandalism but remains one of the most recognized works of art in the world.

1 **S.** The painting depicts a militia company loading up their weapons and preparing to march out.

2 **T.** This militia was led by Captain Frans Banning Cocq as well as his lieutenant, Willem van Ruytenburch.

4 **U.** Due to changing styles in painting, Rembrandt's popularity declined not long after the Night Watch was completed.

~~STQRU~~

STQUR

ANSWERS & EXPLANATIONS: TEST TWO

Paragraph 1 (SURTQ)

The topic sentence establishes the theme of the paragraph, which is the Titanic's construction. S starts the story in 1909 with the beginning of its construction. U follows by introducing the thousands of Irish workers who built the ship while establishing that they risked their lives to do so. R gives a statistic about the number of workers who suffered injuries. T gives a further grim fact about the men who died building the Titanic. Q ends the paragraph with the Titanic setting sail for its doomed maiden voyage.

Paragraph 2 (RTQUS)

The topic sentence introduces the film *The Battle of Algiers* and its premise. R elaborates further on the film's premise from the topic sentence. T transitions with how Gillo Pontecorvo went about achieving his vision, and Q provides some specific examples. U discusses the completed film's release as well as the reaction it received, and S ends the paragraph by addressing the picture's legacy.

Paragraph 3 (QSRUT)

The topic sentence introduces the World Chess Championship and explains its purpose. Q follows with the organization's inception and how the rules of the game were determined. S explains how and why the rules of the game changed while introducing another organization called FIDE. R introduces Garry Kasparov and talks about how he broke away from FIDE. U introduces Kasparov's rival organization, while T concludes with Kasparov's defeat and the rivalry ending.

Paragraph 4 (TQRSU)

The topic sentence establishes the difficulties in putting a live sketch comedy show together. T must follow as it explains what the first step is. Q follows with the scripts introduced in T getting approval from the head writer. Then, R has the producers approving of the sketches as turned in by the head writer. S has the actors preparing the finalized scripts, and U concludes with the show's performance.

Paragraph 5 (STQUR)

The topic sentence has Rembrandt van Rijn completing his most famous and recognizable work. S elaborates on the painting itself and its depiction of a militia. T introduces the head of this militia, Frans Banning Cocq as well as its lieutenant. Q follows because it discusses the introduced Banning Cocq commissioning Rembrandt to do the painting in the first place. U comes next as it addresses what happened to Rembrandt after he finished the Night Watch. Finally, R wraps up with the Night Watch's aftermath as well as its current reputation.

———— TEST THREE

PARAGRAPH 1

What image comes to your mind if somebody says the word "battleship"?

_2_ **Q.** The dreadnought was the most commonly used battleship during wartime throughout the early 20th century.

_5_ **R.** In addition, the dreadnought led to an arms race between various world powers until the end of World War I.

_1_ **S.** The particular battleship you are thinking of is most likely that of the dreadnought.

_4_ **T.** Innovations such as this resulted in the dismissal of all prior battle-ships as "pre-dreadnought."

_3_ **U.** This new battleship included the innovation of an "all-big-gun" struc-ture designed to increase the firepower and accuracy of the vessel.

S Q U T R ✓

PARAGRAPH 2

Author H.P. Lovecraft introduced an unusual creature into the world of science-fiction.

_3_ **Q.** Lovecraft gave the creature many bizarre features including wings on its back and a head like an octopus.

_____ **R.** But good luck trying to pronounce its name!

_____ **S.** Although the story was published in 1928, the Cthulhu still inspires the imaginations of science-fiction fans of all ages.

_2_ **T.** In the story, the Cthulhu has been imprisoned in an underwater city and is worshipped all over the world.

_1_ **U.** The Cthulhu appeared in Lovecraft's "The Call of Cthulhu," which was first published in a magazine called Weird Tales.

 Q U T S R ✗

 U T Q S R

★ **FIVE POINTS LEARNING**

PARAGRAPH 3

The hognose snake can be easily recognized by its pig-like snout.

___3___ **Q.** However, it may bite if you happen to smell like its prey.

___4___ **R.** Moreover, you are most likely to find it in the United States as well as parts of Mexico.

___2___ **S.** This hiss usually scares away its predators, and so it rarely bites unless absolutely necessary.

___?___ **T.** If the hognose feels threatened by you, it will rise up and angrily hiss.

___S___ **U.** If you find the hognose snake appealing, you might be able to buy one on the exotic pet market.

T ~~SQRU~~   R T S Q U

PARAGRAPH 4

Ian Dury was one of the most charismatic and unusual performers in the history of rock and roll.

___2___ **Q.** This illness made him determined to work as hard as possible for his success.

___5___ **R.** He continued to defy expectations with his art until he passed away in 2000.

___4___ **S.** This band was known for its blending of different musical styles like jazz and reggae, as well as Dury's eccentric performing style.

___3___ **T.** Dury fronted several bands but the most successful of these was Ian Dury and the Blockheads.

___1___ **U.** As a child, Dury contracted polio and spent two years learning how to walk again.

UQTSR   ✓

PARAGRAPH 5

Sherlock Holmes has remained one of the most popular and most imitated fictional characters of all-time.

_3_ **Q.** Thus, in a story called "The Final Problem," Sherlock Holmes falls off a cliff after an encounter with his nemesis, Professor Moriarty.

_1_ **R.** But Sir Arthur Conan Doyle, Sherlock's creator, did not share the world's enthusiasm.

_5_ **S.** Unfortunately, fans were so devastated that Doyle eventually went back to the stories, resurrecting Sherlock in a collection called "The Return of Sherlock Holmes."

_2_ **T.** Doyle grew tired of writing the Holmes and Watson adventures and devised a plan to end the series once and for all.

_4_ **U.** With Sherlock dead, Doyle believed he could spend his time writing the books that he was more interested in.

R T Q U S

ANSWERS & EXPLANATIONS: TEST THREE

Paragraph 1 (SQUTR)

The topic sentence introduces the battleship in the form of a question. S answers this question by giving the dreadnought a specific type of battleship as an example. Q elaborates on the dreadnought a little further, while U goes even further by discussing one of its innovations. R must follow because of the "innovation" detail and it also concludes the paragraph with the dreadnought's effects.

Paragraph 2 (UTQSR)

The topic sentence introduces H.P. Lovecraft and foreshadows the subject of the paragraph, the Cthulhu. U is the first sentence to mention the Cthulhu and it must come first because it discusses its first appearance within science-fiction. T then gives more information on the story in which the Cthulhu appeared, and then Q addresses the physical details that Lovecraft provided within the story. S follows as it talks about the Cthulhu's legacy after the story was published, while R ends the paragraph with a concluding and arguably humorous thought.

Paragraph 3 (RTSQU)

The topic sentence describes the hognose snake, while sentence R adds its most likely location. All the other sentences concern its defense mechanisms. T introduces the snake's hiss. S follows with the effects of said hiss and whether or not it intends to bite its prey. Q goes into more detail about the snake's bite, explaining that humans are only sometimes at risk. U concludes the paragraph with a suggestion on where to buy it as a pet (Editors Note: You probably need your parents' permission first.)

Paragraph 4 (UQTSR)

The topic sentence establishes Ian Dury as the subject of the paragraph. U follows with Dury's childhood and introduces his illness. Q then addresses Dury's fight with the illness and how it drove him towards his music career. T brings us to Dury's most famous band, the Blockheads. S elaborates on the kind of music that Ian Dury and the Blockheads performed. R concludes with Dury's legacy and his death.

Paragraph 5 (RTQUS)

The topic sentence introduces Sherlock Holmes as a universally loved fictional character. R directly contrasts with Sir Arthur Conan Doyle disliking his own creation. T has Doyle disliking Holmes so much that he decides to get out of writing the stories. Q introduces the story in which Doyle initially killed off Sherlock Holmes. U follows with Doyle deciding to write other works having killed off his most popular character. S concludes the paragraph with Doyle reluctantly going back to the Holmes and Watson stories.

———— TEST FOUR

PARAGRAPH 1

An oil well fire is one of the most dangerous things that can happen within the oil industry.

_1_ **Q.** This is because one of these fires can result in the loss of millions of dollars worth of oil every day.

_2_ **R.** In addition, the amount of smoke released into the atmosphere has harmful consequences for the environment.

_4_ **S.** The most common method for putting it out is to use explosives such as dynamite.

_5_ **T.** The resulting explosion extinguishes the fire by pushing the flames away from the well's path.

_3_ **U.** So, when an oil fire occurs, firefighters need to put it out as quickly as possible.

QRUST ✓

PARAGRAPH 2

The trombone is unique compared to other instruments within the brass family.

_5_ **Q.** However, it was actually Joachim Nicolas Eggert who first used the instrument a year earlier.

_2_ **R.** While most brass instruments create notes by using valves, the trombone hits these notes with a slide.

_4_ **S.** Many people believe that the first composer to incorporate the trombone into one of his symphonies was Ludwig van Beethoven in 1808.

_1_ **T.** The trombone evolved from a common Renaissance instrument called the sackbut.

_3_ **U.** The musician moves the slide up and down in order to play notes at varying pitches.

TRUSQ

RUTSQ X

PARAGRAPH 3

While everybody knows about the groundbreaking work of Thomas Edison, few people know about the equally important work of his rival, Nikola Tesla.

_____ **Q.** None of the wireless technology we rely upon today would be possible were it not for Tesla's inventions and ideas.

_____ **R.** Among his most significant inventions is the Tesla coil.

_____ **S.** The coil is an air transformer that converts low-voltage high current to high-voltage low current at high frequencies.

_____ **T.** Tesla believed the earth to be a conductor of acoustical resonance, and tested out this theory through many of his inventions.

_____ **U.** In doing so, he discovered that the coil emitted electromagnetic waves.

T R S U Q

PARAGRAPH 4

Some people can't tell the difference between the llama and the alpaca.

_____ **Q.** Fiber is similar to the kind of hair that we humans have.

_____ **R.** Also, while the llama is bred for labor, the alpaca is bred for fiber.

_____ **S.** But the alpaca is a much smaller animal than the llama.

_____ **T.** However, unlike our hair, alpaca fiber is used for knitting and weaving.

_____ **U.** This material is similar to wool but is considered warmer and softer, and increasingly more popular as a fabric.

S R Q T U

PARAGRAPH 5

Have you ever tried to write something with a rock?

_4_ **Q.** The most notable of these chalk cliffs are the White Cliffs of Dover in the south of England.

_2_ **R.** Chalk is a type of sedimentary rock known as limestone.

_5_ **S.** Whether from the mountains or the ocean, chalk deposits are constantly mined and honed down into the chalk sticks we use regularly in our classrooms.

_3_ **T.** This type of limestone can be found on the ocean floor in formations known as chalk deposits.

_1_ **U.** Believe it or not, you've probably written with rocks many times.

U R T Q S

ANSWERS & EXPLANATIONS: TEST FOUR

Paragraph 1 (QRUST)

The topic sentence introduces the dangers of an oil fire. Q gives the financial reason for this danger, while R directly transitions into the environmental risks an oil fire poses. U must come next as it shifts the paragraph into how this type of fire is extinguished. S offers up a common means for putting out the fire, while T concludes the paragraph with the final effect of this means.

Paragraph 2 (RUTSQ)

The topic sentence establishes the trombone as a unique instrument amongst other brass instruments. R explains that this crucial difference is a slide as opposed to the valves of others. U then explains how the slide works to produce music from the trombone. The next three sentences explain the trombone's history: T mentions how the trombone evolved into what it is, S suggests its first appearance in a popular symphonic work, but Q provides its actual first appearance.

Paragraph 3 (TRSUQ)

The topic sentence introduces Nikola Tesla as a rival of inventor Thomas Edison. T follows with the philosophy that Tesla would test out through his inventions. R uses the coil as an example of the ideas expressed in T. S elaborates on exactly how the coil works. U follows with the conclusion that Tesla drew from his coil invention. Q concludes with a summary on the underrated importance of Tesla's findings.

Paragraph 4 (SRQTU)

The topic sentence establishes the contrast between the llama and the alpaca. S transitions with the most obvious contrast: their heights. R follows with an additional example, and it also introduces fiber into the paragraph. Q then explains exactly what fiber is and compares it to hair. T then explains a crucial difference between fiber and human hair, which is that the former is used for knitting and weaving. U concludes with additional information about using fiber for this purpose.

Paragraph 5 (URTQS)

The topic sentence poses a question about writing with rock. U answers that question by telling us that we write with rock often. R then introduces chalk, a common writing implement, as a type of rock called limestone. T delivers the location of limestone as that of chalk cliffs. Q then explains where some of these chalk cliffs can be found. S concludes with the journey that chalk makes from the cliffs to the classrooms.

—————— TEST FIVE

PARAGRAPH 1

World War I began when Gavrilo Princip assassinated Archduke Franz Ferdinand in 1914.

_____ **Q.** The Archduke was passing through the streets of Sarajevo in Bosnia on the day of his murder.

_____ **R.** But his assassination almost didn't happen.

_____ **S.** After a bomb misfired, the carriage changed its route and the remaining conspirators gave up.

_____ **T.** However, when Princip accidentally came across the carriage on his way home, he sprang into action and changed the course of history forever.

_____ **U.** Six conspirators, including Princip, were stationed throughout the streets prepared to strike the Archduke's carriage.

PARAGRAPH 2

Millions of ghost stories begin with the phrase, "It was a dark and stormy night."

_____ **Q.** "The pen is mightier than the sword" comes from a play he wrote about Cardinal Richelieu.

_____ **R.** In fact, the line is only the beginning of the book's first sentence.

_____ **S.** Bulwer-Lytton is also the author of another famous phrase.

_____ **T.** The man who came up with this phrase was a novelist called Edward Bulwer-Lytton.

_____ **U.** Bulwer-Lytton wrote it as the first line of his novel, *Paul Clifford*.

PARAGRAPH 3

The Shih Tzu is a breed of dog that holds its origins in China.

_____ **Q.** This is because the Shih Tzu was bred to resemble the guardian lions that so often appear in ancient Chinese art.

_____ **R.** In fact, the name stems from the China's word for "lion dog."

_____ **S.** Despite this, the Shih Tzu actually makes a poor guard dog because it is so friendly.

_____ **T.** Finally, the Shih Tzu typically has a long life, with its average life expectancy at 13 years.

_____ **U.** Nevertheless, its friendly nature means that the Shih Tzu can easily make friends with other dogs.

PARAGRAPH 4

Contrary to popular belief, we have more than five senses.

_____ **Q.** So many other feelings we go through, such as hunger and thirst, count as senses that we don't even realize we have.

_____ **R.** Nociception is the ability to sense pain, no matter how big or small.

_____ **S.** We use these senses – touch, taste, sight, smell, and hearing – to learn information about the environment that we are in.

_____ **T.** For example, most of us possess a sense called nociception.

_____ **U.** But these are far from the only ways in which to gather this information.

PARAGRAPH 5

The American folk music revival hit its stride in the early-to-mid-1960s.

_____ Q. It began twenty years earlier, and evolved from the popularity of other musical genres like country and bluegrass.

_____ R. The most popular of these musicians, such as Bob Dylan and Phil Ochs, primarily wrote protest songs concerning the war in Vietnam.

_____ S. However, the influence of the folk music revival can still be heard in the popular music of today.

_____ T. During its most popular period, several folk musicians traveled to New York City's Greenwich Village and found great success there.

_____ U. The movement may have continued to grow in popularity were it not for the rise of rock and roll around the same time.

ANSWERS & EXPLANATIONS: TEST FIVE

Paragraph 1 (RQUST)

The topic sentence introduces Gavrilo Princip as the instigator of World War I. R contrasts the topic sentence directly with the fact that his assassination of Archduke Franz Ferdinand almost didn't happen. The remaining sentences elaborate on this fact: Q sets the scene of the Archduke's death, U lists Princip amongst six conspirators involved in the assassination, S offers the first failed attempt towards the Archduke's life, and T concludes the paragraph with the chance encounter that resulted in World War I.

Paragraph 2 (TURSQ)

The topic sentence introduces the famous phrase that the paragraph is about. T introduces Edward Bulwer-Lytton as its author. U cites the work in which Bulwer-Lytton first wrote this phrase. R provides the additional fact that the it is only part of a longer sentence. S then introduces a different famous phrase that Bulwer-Lytton wrote, and Q ends the paragraph with the second phrase in question.

Paragraph 3 (RQSUT)

The topic sentence introduces the Shih Tzu and its origins. R follows up with the origin of the dog's name. Q proceeds with the reason behind its name as its relation to guardian lions. S contrasts its name with the notion that it is actually a poor guard dog. U elaborates on the "friendly nature" that was introduced in S, and T wraps up with a statement concerning the Shih Tzu's long life.

Paragraph 4 (SUTRQ)

The topic sentence provides us with a surprising fact about our senses. S discusses the five senses that are often referred to as the only senses we have. U transitions with the notion that we have more than five senses with which to gather information. T introduces nociception as one of these senses. R defines nociception, and Q concludes the paragraph with an indication of other senses we wouldn't necessarily think of.

Paragraph 5 (QTRUS)

The topic sentence establishes the most popular time period for America's folk music revival. Q explains that the revival had started several years before the stride. T goes back to the popularity of the 1960s and lists New York as its thriving location. R mentions some of the popular musicians that were hinted at in T. U offers a possible reason for the fading out of the movement, and S ends the paragraph with its legacy and influence since.

TEST SIX

PARAGRAPH 1

There are three species of the New Zealand wattlebird, only two of which are still around.

_____ **Q.** Its unfortunate extinction is down to two reasons.

_____ **R.** The Huia's extinction also resulted from deforestation, which continues to threaten the lives of animals throughout the world.

_____ **S.** This led to severe overhunting simply because people thought of their skin and feathers as fashion accessories.

_____ **T.** First, Huia were hunted after for their skins as well as their exotic feathers.

_____ **U.** Sadly, the Huia became extinct in the early 20th century.

PARAGRAPH 2

Changing your name in America can either be simple or complicated.

_____ **Q.** This depends on what state in which you are living.

_____ **R.** However, in some states, you may need a court order for the new name to be officially recognized.

_____ **S.** In addition, some places require an explanation as to why to want to change your name at all.

_____ **T.** But as long as you don't plan to change your name to something offensive, you can give yourself any new name you want.

_____ **U.** In most states, you can change your name without any legal difficulties at all.

PARAGRAPH 3

Sir Thomas More was one of the most notable victims of the Reformation of England.

_____ **Q.** As a result, More was executed for treason, only to be recognized as a Catholic martyr many years later.

_____ **R.** Later, More was promoted to Chancellor after the previous Chancellor, Cardinal Wolsey, was removed from the job.

_____ **S.** Early on in his career, More became a personal advisor to King Henry VIII.

_____ **T.** But More, a devout Catholic, openly disapproved of the new marriage as well as Henry's breaking away from the Catholic church.

_____ **U.** Henry believed that Wolsey was trying to prevent the King's divorce and subsequent marriage to Anne Boleyn.

PARAGRAPH 4

People all over the world like to start the day either with coffee or tea.

_____ **Q.** But a debate rages on as to which caffeinated beverage contains more antioxidants, which are important because they assist in maintaining a healthy body.

_____ **R.** This is mainly because both drinks contain caffeine, which provides the drinker with a boost of energy in the morning.

_____ **S.** In the end, it just depends on which caffeinated beverage you personally prefer.

_____ **T.** That said, people who drink six to eight cups of tea a day are getting far more antioxidants than those who only drink up to two cups of coffee a day.

_____ **U.** On the one hand, one cup of coffee contains more antioxidants than does one cup of tea.

PARAGRAPH 5

A face transplant is necessary when severe damage is done to a person's face.

_____ **Q.** Dinoire underwent the operation after she suffered an attack from her dog.

_____ **R.** France's Isabelle Dinoire received the first partial face transplant in 2005.

_____ **S.** Two years later, a detailed report confirmed that the operation was indeed a success.

_____ **T.** This damage can affect somebody's entire face or only some of it in order for a transplant to become necessary.

_____ **U.** Meanwhile, the first successful transplant of an entire face took place years later in Spain.

ANSWERS & EXPLANATIONS: TEST SIX

Paragraph 1 (UQTSR)

The topic sentence establishes the only three species of New Zealand wattlebird, one of which is extinct. R offers the name of the extinct species. Q then sets up two reasons for the Huia's extinction. U transitions into the first reason while S elaborates further on that reason. T ends the paragraph with the second reason.

Paragraph 2 (QURST)

The topic sentence introduces the process of changing your name as either simple or complicated. Q attributes this distinction to the different U.S. states. U provides a generalization about the rules of most states in this regard. R contrasts the majority of states with some exceptions. S then provides an additional require-ment for these states. T concludes by reassuring you that most name changes will be deemed acceptable except in extreme cases.

Paragraph 3 (SRUTQ)

The topic sentence recognizes Sir Thomas More as a crucial figure in English history. S addresses part of his early career as well as his relationship with Henry VIII. R talks about his promotion to Chancellor later on in his career after the sacking of Cardinal Wolsey. U explains that Wolsey was removed for meddling in Henry's marriage to Anne Boleyn. T elaborates on the marriage with More's disapproval due to religious reasons. Q ends the paragraph with More's execution "as a result" of his disapproval.

Paragraph 4 (RQUTS)

The topic sentence sets up the paragraph as a comparison between coffee and tea. R transitions with the reason that both beverages are so popular in the morning. Q comes next as it's the first sentence to bring up the debate over the drinks' health. U leads with "on the one hand" and the pro-coffee argument. T must follow as it provides the pro-tea argument, leading with "that said." S concludes with the debate still unresolved.

Paragraph 5 (TRQSU)

The topic sentence introduces the notion of a face transplant. T elaborates on the level of damage as addressed in the topic sentence. R introduces Isabelle Dinoire as the first recipient of a successful face transplant. Q provides more background as to Dinoire's operation. S comes next with the aftermath of the operation a couple years later. U wraps up with the first full face transplant some time after that.

——— TEST SEVEN

PARAGRAPH 1

Monopoly has arguably been America's most beloved board game of the 20th century.

_____ **Q.** Magie's game involved players moving around the board and buying up land.

_____ **R.** Her goal was to demonstrate the process of buying land as well as its consequences both good and bad.

_____ **S.** Its origins date back to 1903 when a woman named Elizabeth Magie created a game called *The Landlord's Game*.

_____ **T.** Several games followed that recreated both its premise and its process.

_____ **U.** But in 1936, a toy company called Parker Brothers released *Monopoly*, which outsold and outlasted them all.

PARAGRAPH 2

Photosynthesis is a process by which plants convert sunlight into energy and release oxygen into the earth's atmosphere.

_____ **Q.** Lab experiments in artificial photosynthesis have been successful so far, but there is much more work to do before it is ready for the masses

_____ **R.** Still, scientists hope that this may bring clean energy to the world once and for all.

_____ **S.** Not only must the converter be able to harvest sunlight, but it must also have the ability to split water molecules.

_____ **T.** In order for artificial photosynthesis to work, an energy converter needs to be able to undertake two procedures.

_____ **U.** While this is a natural process, scientists have been investigating the possibilities of artificial photosynthesis.

PARAGRAPH 3

Most film directors rely on special effects in order to create movie magic.

_____ **Q.** The result was one of cinema's most striking images, and proof that you don't always need special effects to dazzle an audience.

_____ **R.** For example, Werner Herzog's *Fitzcarraldo* tells the story of a wealthy man who took a steam ship to the Peruvian jungles in order to access and sell rubber.

_____ **S.** In one famous sequence, the ship is pulled all the way over a mountain.

_____ **T.** However, sometimes they go to extreme measures to achieve their visions on screen.

_____ **U.** Herzog rejected effects and had his crew film the real ship going over a real mountain.

PARAGRAPH 4

The Pinto is a car that the Ford Motor Company would probably like everyone to forget.

_____ **Q.** Notoriously, if the car suffered a rear-end collision, the fuel tank was likely to explode.

_____ **R.** Throughout the Pinto's production during this decade, drivers across America purchased well over 3 million.

_____ **S.** After many fatalities and lawsuits, Ford discontinued the Pinto, its legacy now living in infamy.

_____ **T.** Despite its success, the Pinto's reputation has fared badly in recent years.

_____ **U.** This was a subcompact car that was first released in the early 1970s.

PARAGRAPH 5

The slow loris is a nocturnal primate that dwells within the jungles of Indonesia.

_____ **Q.** This makes the slow loris the only poisonous primate in existence.

_____ **R.** In order to defend itself, the slow loris comes with a bite that unleashes toxins that can prove deadly to some beings, including humans.

_____ **S.** Also known as the night monkey, this is an omnivore that slowly inches towards its prey before attacking suddenly.

_____ **T.** Fortunately, animal rescue teams around the world have intervened to protect the slow loris from poachers and finally reverse its endangerment.

_____ **U.** Sadly, the slow loris is also among the 25 most endangered primates in the world.

ANSWERS & EXPLANATIONS: TEST SEVEN

Paragraph 1 (SQRTU)

The topic sentence introduces the board game *Monopoly* and its popularity. S talks about its origins in a different game created by Elizabeth Magie. Q elaborates on how Magie's game worked. R takes this further with Magie's intentions behind the game. T addresses the game's influence on others, while U concludes the paragraph with the inception of the most popular of these games, *Monopoly.*

Paragraph 2 (UTSQR)

The topic sentence defines the natural process of photosynthesis. U introduces the notion of artificial photosynthesis. T addresses how artificial photosynthesis has to work via an energy converter, while S elaborates on the functionality of the energy converter. Q provides a statement on the progress of artificial photosynthesis. R concludes the paragraph with the possibility of artificial photosynthesis providing clean energy to all.

Paragraph 3 (TRSUQ)

The topic sentence attributes special effects as to how most movies are made. T transitions into another way of making movie magic. R introduces a film by Werner Herzog as an example of an unusual moviemaking method. S provides one of the film's more famous sequences involving a boat and a mountain. U explains that Herzog actually dragged the boat over the mountain rather than rely on special effects. Q wraps up the paragraph by concluding that special effects aren't the only way of dazzling audiences.

Paragraph 4 (URTQS)

The topic sentence introduces the Ford Pinto. U provides the decade in which the Pinto was released to the public. R offers a statistic that relates to the initial success of the car. T transitions from its positive reputation at the time to its negative reputation now. Q provides the fatal reason for its bad reputation these days. S concludes with the discontinuation of the Pinto after many fatalities and lawsuits.

Paragraph 5 (SRQUT)

The topic sentence introduces and defines the slow loris. S comes next as it is the first sentence to address its method of attack. R follows with the poisonous nature of its bite, which is also a defense mechanism. Q uses the fact about the poison to explain that the creature is the only poisonous primate around. U transitions into its status as endangered, but T ends the paragraph on a positive note with rescue teams assisting in the survival of the slow loris.

—————— TEST EIGHT

PARAGRAPH 1

The Four Corners region is a unique spot within the United States' geography.

_____ **Q.** There is nowhere else in America in which the borders of four states meet.

_____ **R.** This spot is known as a quadripoint because it brings together the borders of four different regions.

_____ **S.** Today, the monument is one of America's major tourist attractions.

_____ **T.** To commemorate this unique fact, a Four Corners monument was established in 1931.

_____ **U.** The quadripoint in question connects the borders of Colorado, New Mexico, Utah, and Arizona.

PARAGRAPH 2

The works of William Shakespeare remain the most respected, read, and performed plays in all of Western civilization.

_____ **Q.** However, some people believe that Shakespeare didn't write any of his plays.

_____ **R.** These skeptics have suggested that other playwrights like Christopher Marlowe and Francis Bacon used the name of William Shakespeare to avoid credit for their works.

_____ **S.** This theory stems partly from the fact that much about Shakespeare's life remains a mystery to this day.

_____ **T.** Nevertheless, the theory remains an unpopular view, and most people continue to believe that Shakespeare was a real man who indeed wrote such classic plays as *Hamlet* and *King Lear*.

_____ **U.** In addition, skeptics believe that his mysterious life is inconsistent with the reputation he had as a brilliant and popular playwright.

PARAGRAPH 3

There is a list of Chinese novels commonly referred to as the Four Great Classical Novels.

_____ **Q.** One of the four novels is Wu Cheng'en's *Journey to the West.*

_____ **R.** Cheng'en's original text is a hundred chapters and is one of the longest novels in the history of literature.

_____ **S.** In addition, his work has lived on in popular culture through the mediums of television and even opera.

_____ **T.** This book tells the story of a monk who takes a pilgrimage towards India alongside the Monkey King.

_____ **U.** These novels are notable because of their influence of modern Chinese literature.

PARAGRAPH 4

Subletting is a real estate practice in which an existing tenant allows a third party to stay in his or her quarters.

_____ **Q.** The subtenant is responsible for paying rent and following the terms of the lease until the tenant returns.

_____ **R.** This makes the third party the subtenant.

_____ **S.** But subletting doesn't only apply to houses or apartments.

_____ **T.** If the tenant has to go out of town, the landlord may allow the tenant to sublet for a temporary period of time.

_____ **U.** For instance, companies have the right to sublet office space as long as they have the landlord's consent.

PARAGRAPH 5

Many historians believe that the Renaissance began when the printing press was invented.

_____ Q. That all changed when Johannes Gutenberg unveiled his printing press in the middle of the 15th century

_____ R. Before this invention, rewriting the words into new books with pen and ink was the only way to make copies of books for distribution.

_____ S. In addition, it became easier to translate books, which led to different versions of the Bible circulating throughout Europe.

_____ T. Gutenberg's invention enabled editors to fill over 250 letters with ink and press down the formed words onto paper.

_____ U. Now, books could be copied at a much faster rate.

ANSWERS & EXPLANATIONS: TEST EIGHT

Paragraph 1 (RUQST)

The topic sentence introduces the tourist attraction called the Four Corners. R defines the attraction further and gives it the term, "quadripoint." U explains what a quadripoint is and how it relates to the Four Corners and the states it represents. Q offers the additional fact about these four states and how unique they are. S transitions into the Four Corners becoming a monument to commemorate this fact, and T ends with a summary of the Four Corner's as a tourist attraction.

Paragraph 2 (QSURT)

The topic sentence summarizes the reputation of William Shakespeare and his plays. Q transitions into the conspiracy that Shakespeare may not have actually written his plays. S gives a reason for why this controversial theory came about in the first place. U then provides an additional fact along these lines. R responds to S and U by offering alternate playwrights as the sources of these famous works. T wraps up by concluding that the conspiracy theory remains largely dismissed.

Paragraph 3 (UQTRS)

The topic sentence introduces China's Four Great Classical Novels. U elaborates on why the four novels have this outstanding reputation. Q transitions into one of these novels as well as its author. T then summarizes the plot of this particular novel. R provides an additional fact about the novel, and S ends the paragraph with its reputation in popular culture.

Paragraph 4 (TRQSU)

The topic sentence defines the practice of subletting. T elaborates on the definition by explaining why subletting might be necessary for some. R introduces the subtenant who would take part in the scenario that was explained in R. Next, Q explains the responsibilities of the subtenant until the tenant returns. S moves the paragraph away from subletting apartments, and U follows with another example of subletting.

Paragraph 5 (RQTUS)

The topic sentence offers the theory that the Renaissance kicked off with the invention of the printing press. R comes next as it explains what publishing was like before the printing press came along. Q transitions to the press with the phrase "that all changed," and then introduces Johannes Gutenberg as its inventor. T explains how Gutenberg's invention worked. U follows with the results of the invention. S concludes the paragraph with another long-term effect of the printing press.

TEST NINE

PARAGRAPH 1

Spalding Gray was an actor who decided to turn his own life into art.

_____ **Q.** While growing up in Rhode Island, Gray developed an interest in theatre and, in particular, acting.

_____ **R.** Gray drew upon his personal experiences and was always totally honest about himself.

_____ **S.** Gray's monologues would transform the nature of theatre and continue to inspire performers to this day.

_____ **T.** He moved to New York City where he began acting professionally and even helped found an independent theatre company.

_____ **U.** After a while, Gray became bored with the theatre he was doing and started writing his own monologues.

PARAGRAPH 2

Rugby is a sport that enjoys popularity throughout the United Kingdom and Ireland.

_____ **Q.** In the middle of the game, Ellis allegedly picked up the ball with his hands and ran with it.

_____ **R.** In 1823, an Englishman called William Webb Ellis was playing a game of soccer.

_____ **S.** This moment deliberately went against the soccer rules, and as soon as he did it, the game of rugby was born.

_____ **T.** Although this story has never been confirmed, it demonstrates a key distinction between soccer and rugby, and may explain why the latter is preferred among certain athletes.

_____ **U.** It is not known how rugby came about, but one origins story remains the most accepted.

PARAGRAPH 3

When World War II ended, several nations struggled to rebuild and find a new global identity for themselves.

_____ **Q.** In the middle of the four zones, the center of Vienna constituted an international zone, which was used for negotiations between the nations.

_____ **R.** One such nation was Vienna, which had been badly bombed out during the conflict.

_____ **S.** These zones were controlled by the United States, France, Great Britain, and Soviet Russia, respectively.

_____ **T.** After the war finally drew to a close, Vienna's government was divided into four occupied zones.

_____ **U.** Vienna's fractured state of being continued until all four powers pulled out of the country over the next ten years.

PARAGRAPH 4

The Brothers Karamazov was the final novel written by the Russian novelist Fyodor Dostoevsky.

_____ **Q.** Although Dostoevsky died before the book was published, he left behind an epic work that many consider his great masterpiece.

_____ **R.** These motivations come from their unique character traits, which is how Dostoevsky explores the themes that troubled him all his life.

_____ **S.** Throughout his career, Dostoevsky wrote books that explored ideas of spirituality and morals.

_____ **T.** All four brothers have separate motivations for the murder of the father.

_____ **U.** In this book, he explores these themes through four brothers and their father whom they greatly admire.

PARAGRAPH 5

A mirage is an optical illusion in which ripples of water suddenly appear before your very eyes.

_____ **Q.** For example, light can bend as it passes from a colder kind of air to a warmer kind.

_____ **R.** This transition gives off the effect that water ripples are glazing over whatever it is that your eyes are observing.

_____ **S.** But these mirages are mere hallucinations and are only temporary.

_____ **T.** This illusion is typically created through light refractions.

_____ **U.** In light refractions, light bends from one state to another state.

ANSWERS & EXPLANATIONS: TEST NINE

Paragraph 1 (QTURS)

The topic sentence introduces the actor and artist Spalding Gray. Q follows with Gray's background and how it led to his acting career. T comes next as it has Gray moving to New York to pursue his acting ambitions. U transitions into Gray's boredom with theatre, thereby leading to his monologues. R elaborates on what his monologues were like. S concludes the paragraph with the legacy of his work.

Paragraph 2 (URQST)

The topic sentence introduces rugby and its popularity. U transitions into a discussion on the sport's mysterious origins. R follows with one possible theory involving William Webb Ellis, a 19th-century soccer player. Q then provides an action that he performed in the middle of a soccer game. S comes to the conclusion that this action spontaneously created rugby. T wraps up the paragraph by defining the story as a key distinction between rugby and soccer.

Paragraph 3 (RTSQU)

The topic sentence begins the paragraph with World War II's grim aftermath for many nations. R gives Vienna as an example of one of these nations. T follows with Vienna being divided up into four zones after the war ended. S then lists all the nations that required these zones. Q comes next, describing the one area that wasn't controlled by the four powers and how they exploited it. U ends the paragraph with the nations finally leaving several years later.

Paragraph 4 (SUTRQ)

The topic sentence is about Fyodor Dostoevsky's last novel. S follows by examining the themes within the novels that he wrote up until *Karamazov*. U ties this final book in with those other works. T then explains the plot of the novel while R elaborates on how the plot represents Dostoevsky's reoccurring themes. Q ends with Dostoevsky's death and the legacy of his final work.

Paragraph 5 (TUQRS)

The topic sentence defines a mirage as an optical illusion. T follows as it explains that the illusion comes about via light refractions. U elaborates on light refractions and depicts them as transitions of light from one state to another. Q provides a specific example of how the transition takes effect. R goes into the effect that the light refractions have to create the mirages we can see. S concludes by downplaying mirages as temporary hallucinations.

TEST TEN

PARAGRAPH 1

The Salvation Army is among the most recognizable charity organizations in the world.

_____ **Q.** The mission of these Salvationists was to bring salvation to the poor and the suffering.

_____ **R.** Today, there are Salvation Armies all over the world continuing on the mission that the Booths started so many years ago.

_____ **S.** For instance, William Booth made himself General of the organization and ranked those below him as officers and soldiers called Salvationists.

_____ **T.** Unlike other charities, the Salvation Army was structured like a military operation.

_____ **U.** William and Catherine Booth founded the first Salvation Army in London in the 19th century.

PARAGRAPH 2

After Lewis and Clark's famous expedition across America, several trails from one region to another sprouted up to explore the resources of this newly acquired land.

_____ **Q.** In its early days, the Oregon Trail was only passable by horseback or by simply walking.

_____ **R.** One of these expeditions was two thousand miles long and took travelers from Missouri all the way up to Oregon.

_____ **S.** Although the Oregon Trail is no longer necessary, many highways and other routes follow a similar path and therefore keep the legacy of the journey alive.

_____ **T.** As technology improved, it became commonplace to take ox-drawn wagons on the journey to Oregon.

_____ **U.** This journey became known as the Oregon Trail.

PARAGRAPH 3

Every day, swarms of people go out and buy lottery tickets for themselves.

_____ **Q.** They do this because they dream of becoming a millionaire overnight.

_____ **R.** But some believe that winning the lottery is more of a nightmare than a dream.

_____ **S.** Some of these winners became the targets of financial scams while others lost all their winnings by spending them too quickly.

_____ **T.** Many who have gone on to win a lottery jackpot have been met with terrible luck later on.

_____ **U.** Still, that hasn't stopped the masses from buying lottery tickets and chasing after those jackpots.

PARAGRAPH 4

Oscar Wilde is responsible for some of the English language's most memorable quotes and sayings.

_____ **Q.** Early on in his career, Wilde worked primarily as an essayist and journalist.

_____ **R.** As an adult, Wilde traveled to London to pursue a career as a writer.

_____ **S.** He was born in Dublin, Ireland to a family of intellectuals in 1854.

_____ **T.** In the last ten years of his life, Wilde completed his two most famous works: The *Picture of Dorian Gray* and *The Importance of Being Earnest*.

_____ **U.** In addition, he transformed himself into a colorful and charismatic public personality.

PARAGRAPH 5

Fugu is a Japanese species of fish that poses a unique challenge to seafood chefs.

_____ **Q.** Therefore, Japanese law requires an extensive and exhaustive training process so that only select few chefs are qualified to prepare fugu in restaurants.

_____ **R.** Tetrodotoxin is so poisonous that it doesn't even have an antidote

_____ **S.** Feel free to try some fugu the next time you travel to Japan, but do so at your own risk!

_____ **T.** If this fish is not prepared properly, it has the power to kill its diner with just one bite.

_____ **U.** This is because fugu contains an alarming amount of tetrodotoxin.

ANSWERS & EXPLANATIONS: TEST TEN

Paragraph 1 (UTSQR)

The topic sentence introduces the Salvation Army as well as its reputation. U follows with the creators of the organization back in the 19th century. T contrasts it with other charities by likening it to a military operation. S provides a specific example for how it resembled a military operation and introduces the Salvationists. Q elaborates further on the Salvationists. R concludes with the Salvation Army's current standing in society.

Paragraph 2 (RUQTS)

The topic sentence establishes the many trails that followed Lewis and Clark's expedition. R must follow because it paints a picture of one such journey. U defines the journey as that of the Oregon Trail. Q describes the conditions of the Oregon Trail early on, while T describes it after technological advances. S wraps up by putting the Oregon Trail into a contemporary context.

Paragraph 3 (QRTSU)

The topic sentence introduces the insane popularity of the lottery. Q explains why it is that so many people buy lottery tickets on a regular basis. R offers an alternate opinion that winning the lottery is a dangerous thing. T elaborates that many have suffered misfortune after winning. S follows because it gives specific examples of misfortune. U concludes by stating that this hasn't prevented people from buying lottery tickets.

Paragraph 4 (SRQUT)

The topic sentence introduces and celebrates the life and work of Oscar Wilde. S follows with the context of his early life and upbringing. R transitions into his adult life as an aspiring writer. Q then explores his earliest works. U addresses his personal reputation and how it relates to his writings. T ends by highlighting Wilde's most famous works.

Paragraph 5 (TURQS)

The topic sentence establishes fugu as a challenge to chefs. T gives the deadly reason for this challenge. U elaborates on this challenge by introducing the poison called tetrodotoxin. R explains further just how dangerous tetrodotoxin is. Q comes next with a conclusion on how serious it is to be able to prepare fugu. S ends the paragraph with a warning on anyone thinking of trying the fish.

———— TEST ELEVEN

PARAGRAPH 1

Gonzo journalism was phrase coined to describe a new kind of journalism that arose in the 1970s.

_____ **Q.** For example, an objective journalist never expresses his or her opinion and sticks to the facts instead.

_____ **R.** Meanwhile, the gonzo journalists never pretended to be unbiased and made their opinions perfectly clear in their coverage.

_____ **S.** In addition, gonzo journalism often relied on expressive and emotional language in order to convey an emotional appeal.

_____ **T.** Before then, journalists were expected to maintain their objectivity in reporting the news.

_____ **U.** Gonzo journalism didn't last as a movement but its effects on journalism can still be found in today's news coverage.

PARAGRAPH 2

One of the most famous exports of the Harlem Renaissance movement was Langston Hughes.

_____ **Q.** This led to Hughes' recognition as a major black poet.

_____ **R.** As a child, Hughes displayed a talent for poetry and was even recognized by his school as the class poet.

_____ **S.** Nevertheless, the African-American Hughes felt the effects of being stereotyped by his classmates and carried that with him throughout his life.

_____ **T.** Years later, while working as a busboy, Hughes started getting his poetry published in literary magazines.

_____ **U.** During the peak of his career as a poet, Hughes did most of his work in Harlem and became the great Harlem Renaissance figure we speak of today.

PARAGRAPH 3

Nowadays, one can take a great family photo by holding up a phone and clicking a button.

_____ **Q.** This is because it took about 10 minutes to expose enough natural light into the camera for the daguerrotype to work.

_____ **R.** Louis-Jacques-Mandé Daguerre invented this photographic process in 1837.

_____ **S.** In the beginning, Daguerre's invention was most commonly used to capture landscapes and still-lifes.

_____ **T.** It wouldn't be long before daguerrotypes were used to capture humans as well, and many of the portraits we recognize from the 19th century came to life through Daguerre's creation.

_____ **U.** But photography never would have begun without the invention of the daguerrotype.

PARAGRAPH 4

Petra is the name of an ancient architectural marvel in Jordan.

_____ **Q.** The entire city was carved from rock within the natural landscape.

_____ **R.** Once a major trading city, Petra is now one of the biggest tourist attractions in the Middle East.

_____ **S.** This incredible feat was undertaken by the Nabataeans in 312 BC.

_____ **T.** The Nabataeans had settled there long beforehand and needed a major center for their trading.

_____ **U.** Among the most impressive sites that they built within Petra is Al-Khazneh, or "Treasury," which is thirty meters wide and over forty meters tall.

PARAGRAPH 5

Try to imagine a time when there was no such thing as a sandwich.

_____ **Q.** Little did he know that people all over the world would enjoy variations on the sandwich for the thousands of years to follow.

_____ **R.** After Hillel's death, it became customary during Passover to eat this kind of sandwich and say a prayer honoring the old sage.

_____ **S.** This popular meal has been around so long that we can trace its origins back to ancient Judaism.

_____ **T.** Hillel's sandwich consisted of two pieces of matzah with meat and bitter herbs in between.

_____ **U.** A Jewish sage called Hillel the Elder, who lived between 110 BCE and 10 CE, made the very first sandwich as part of a Passover ceremony.

ANSWERS & EXPLANATIONS: TEST ELEVEN

Paragraph 1 (TQRSU)

The topic sentence introduces the form of journalism known as "gonzo." T follows with a statement on what journalism was like before gonzo journalism came along. Q elaborates on this distinction further. R transitions into the gonzo journalists and how they differed from traditional journalists. S provides an additional fact about gonzo journalism's overall style. U summarizes the long-term effects of gonzo journalism's impact.

Paragraph 2 (RSTQU)

The topic sentence introduces the Harlem Renaissance and the subject of this paragraph, Langston Hughes. R comes next with a description of Hughes' early childhood and interest in poetry. S moves into the personal and cultural stereotyping that he felt in childhood and transitions the paragraph into his adulthood. T follows with Hughes' first published works. Q tells us that "this led to" his growing reputation as a poet. U concludes the paragraph with his legacy and reputation beyond his life.

Paragraph 3 (URSQT)

The topic sentence creates a context for how photographs are taken today. U must follow because it brings the reader back to the origins of today's photography: the daguerrotype. R provides the name of the inventor and the year in which it was created. S explains how his invention was initially used. Q provides a reason for the daguerrotype's specific uses as stated in S. T wraps up with the daguerrotype being embraced for portraits.

Paragraph 4 (QSTUR)

The topic sentence introduces Petra in Jordan. Q explains exactly what Petra is and how it was created. S then identifies the people who built Petra in 312 BC. T follows with an explanation as to why these people created Petra in the first place. U comes next with an example of one of the notable sites within their city. R concludes with Petra's current standing as a major tourist attraction.

Paragraph 5 (SUTRQ)

The topic sentence provides a rhetorical statement about a time without the sandwich. S follows because it responds to the topic sentence with how long the sandwich has been around. U comes next because it starts to elaborate on its origins in ancient Judaism as mentioned in S, and introduces Hillel as its creator. T describes what Hillel's sandwich was like. R mentions what happened to the sandwich after Hillel's death, and Q wraps up the paragraph with the sandwich becoming a common, everyday meal.

——— TEST TWELVE

PARAGRAPH 1

In addition to being one of the greatest film directors of all-time, Orson Welles enjoyed life as a magician and as a prankster.

_____ **Q.** Wells' novel tells the story of an alien invasion that targets local communities.

_____ **R.** Welles took this idea and created a radio program that was being interrupted by fake news bulletins announcing a similar alien attack.

_____ **S.** The broadcast was so effective that many listeners believed the invasion was real, and were outraged when they discovered the hoax shortly after.

_____ **T.** This incident would secure Orson Welles' reputation as one of the 20th century's greatest artists.

_____ **U.** The most notorious of these pranks came about in 1938 when Welles adapted H.G. Wells' _War of the Worlds_ into a radio play.

PARAGRAPH 2

Bloomsday is the most significant Irish holiday that you may not have heard of.

_____ **Q.** All this is recognized every Bloomsday when swarms of literature fans gather in Dublin to celebrate the author and his great masterpiece.

_____ **R.** Bloomsday is held on this date because Joyce's novel takes place on the same day.

_____ **S.** Bloomsday takes place on June 16 every year and it commemorates the writing of _Ulysses_.

_____ **T.** The name of the holiday is a reference to the book's lead character, Leo Bloom.

_____ **U.** _Ulysses_ was written by James Joyce in 1904 and went on to change literature in the English language single-handedly.

PARAGRAPH 3

All cars contain a battery that supplies the electrical energy necessary to get a vehicle moving.

_____ **Q.** As long as the two batteries have the same voltage, you can connect them using jumper cables.

_____ **R.** To jump a battery, you need another car whose battery is functioning properly.

_____ **S.** Once the cables connect the two, you have to start on the functioning car and let it sit idle while the other battery gets its energy back.

_____ **T.** Sometimes, however, batteries need an energy boost in order to get the car working again.

_____ **U.** The process of achieving this boost is most commonly referred to as jumping a battery.

PARAGRAPH 4

Who was the first President of the United States?

_____ **Q.** While Washington was the first President under the United States Constitution, many historians maintain that the first American President was a gentleman by the name of John Hanson.

_____ **R.** Before you answer George Washington, this is actually a trick question.

_____ **S.** Therefore, on a technicality, Hanson can claim himself President before even Washington.

_____ **T.** When the Articles of Confederation was drafted in 1781, Hanson was elected President of the Continental Congress and served a one-year term.

_____ **U.** Hanson had been a Maryland delegate for the Continental Congress that would sign the Declaration of Independence in 1776.

PARAGRAPH 5

When a star reaches the end of its life, it may explode through the cosmos in a burst of light and energy.

_____ **Q.** The stars that go through supernovas are larger than other stars, which may merely burn out.

_____ **R.** When there is nothing left to consume, the star unleashes itself into a supernova that can outshine surrounding stars for the months to come.

_____ **S.** This explosion is known as a supernova.

_____ **T.** This is because the larger stars have spent their existences relying on themselves for fuel to stay burning.

_____ **U.** Occasionally, these stars may suck in other stars for extra fuel.

ANSWERS & EXPLANATIONS: TEST TWELVE

Paragraph 1 (UQRST)

The topic sentence establishes a contrast between Orson Welles the artist and Orson Welles the prankster. U follows by introducing his *War of the Worlds* radio show as an example of one of those pranks. Q provides a plot summary to give the prank some context. R then explains how Welles took the plot and adapted it into a radio show. S describes the effect that Welles' radio program had on the masses. T summarizes the paragraph by drawing a positive conclusion about Welles' reputation.

Paragraph 2 (SURTQ)

The topic sentence introduces the Irish holiday known as Bloomsday. S provides its date and its reason for existence as due to the book *Ulysses.* U elaborates on the book, its author, and its significance. R follows by connecting the book and the holiday. T provides an additional detail that explains the connection between the two. Q ties all of the above together with a summary of Bloomsday's festivities.

Paragraph 3 (TURQS)

The topic sentence introduces the car battery. T follows by explaining that batteries occasionally need to be restarted, and U coins this process as "jumping a battery." The remaining sentences elaborate on how jumping a battery works: R brings the functioning vehicle into the picture, Q has the two cars linked together via jumper cables, and S concludes by explaining how the connection will jump the malfunctioning battery.

Paragraph 4 (RQUTS)

The topic sentence asks a question about the first President of the U.S. R answers this question directly by dismissing the George Washington answer. Q then explains that the first President was not Washington but John Hanson. U gives a background on who Hanson was in the early stages of the American Revolution. T has Hanson's election under the U.S. Articles of Confederation. S summarizes this fact about Hanson as a technicality.

Paragraph 5 (SQTUR)

The topic sentence talks about the end of a star's life via an explosion. S then defines this explosion as a supernova. Q then provides a contrast between stars that go through supernovas and those that don't. T follows by explaining why certain stars are capable of supernovas and others aren't. U provides an additional fact about why it is that the larger stars mentioned in T can expand. R concludes the paragraph with the supernova finally taking place.

—— TEST THIRTEEN

PARAGRAPH 1

Birchbark canoes were traditionally used by the Woodland Indian tribes of North America.

_____ **Q.** The effectiveness of the Birchbark canoe's design is demonstrated by its continued use; today's canoes are an aluminum version of the Woodland Indian's original design.

_____ **R.** These large boats were mainly used for traveling and hunting which made it imperative that they be carried through the woods from one body of water to another.

_____ **S.** Because of this necessity, the boats needed to be lightweight and sturdy enough to carry large animals.

_____ **T.** In order to achieve this effect, canoe builders spent years constructing these unique vessels.

_____ **U.** A finished canoe could carry close to one ton, yet could be hoisted onto a man's shoulder and carried through the woods with ease.

PARAGRAPH 2

Dr. David Livingstone was a great explorer during the Victorian Era.

_____ **Q.** After contracting an illness, Livingstone lost contact with the outside world for six years until *The New York Herald* sent Henry Morton Stanley to locate and urge him to return home.

_____ **R.** He was born in Scotland in 1813, and as a young man became a minister.

_____ **S.** During this time of religious exploration, Livingstone embarked on his first journey to Africa in the hopes of establishing trade and ending slavery.

_____ **T.** Livingstone refused to leave and Stanley joined him on a journey to identify the source of the Nile

_____ **U.** On his second expedition, Livingstone explored the African interior in order to establish trade routes.

PARAGRAPH 3

The game of Cricket originated in England over 300 years ago.

_____ **Q.** This rise in popularity led to the Code of 1744 which established consistent rules for the game.

_____ **R.** Even after the Code was established, the game continued to evolve and is now played worldwide.

_____ **S.** The game began on sheep pastures; shepherds defended a goal as their opponents rolled rags or wool toward a target.

_____ **T.** Although the basic premise was the same, each region that played Cricket developed their own variation of the game.

_____ **U.** In the 1600's, Cricket became so popular the government handed out fines if any person was caught playing Cricket instead of attending their Sunday church services.

PARAGRAPH 4

Many of World War I's biggest battles took place not in the trenches but in the sky.

_____ **Q.** These battles among fighter pilots almost always resulted in the pilots achieving just a few victories before getting shot down.

_____ **R.** One fighter pilot, known as the Red Baron, was the exception with 80 confirmed victories credited to his name.

_____ **S.** At the height of his fighting, Richthofen painted his fighter plane red as the legend around him grew.

_____ **T.** His real name was Manfred von Richthofen, and he served the Imperial German Army Air Service throughout the war.

_____ **U.** The day after his 80th victory, his plane was brought down and the iconic Red Baron was killed at the age of 25.

PARAGRAPH 5

Louis Braille was born in Couprvray, France in 1809.

_____ **Q.** Louis figured out the code quickly and adapted it so it could be used to publish books for the blind.

_____ **R.** When he was three years old, Braille suffered an accident in his father's workshop and hurt his eyes; unfortunately, the wound became infected and Louis became blind in both eyes.

_____ **S.** In 1821, a former soldier visited the school and taught the students "night writing," a special raised code used on the battlefield that allowed soldiers relay secret information silently.

_____ **T.** This efficient system became known as Braille, and It is now used around the world.

_____ **U.** Because of his loss of vision, Braille's parents sent the young boy to attend the Royal Institution for Blind Youth in Paris.

ANSWERS & EXPLANATIONS: TEST THIRTEEN

Paragraph 1 (RSTUQ)

The given sentence introduces birchbark canoes as used by the Woodland Indian tribes of North America. Sentence R follows giving the purpose of these canoes and explains why they needed to be light enough to be carried by one person. S follows R beginning with, "Birchbarks also..." and states that these vessels also had to be sturdy. T then explains that because of these specifications (lightness and sturdiness) the canoes took great skill to build. U then follows to describe the abilities of the finished canoe. Q concludes with the statement that the original design still continues to be used today.

Paragraph 2 (RSUQT)

The topic introduces Dr. David Livingstone as a great explorer. R follows giving his date of birth and his decision to become a minister leading to his first trip to Africa. U leads with, "On his second expedition..." going on to describe this excursion. S then tells of Livingstone's disappearance and Stanley's search for him. Q then explains that Stanley joined Livingstone on a journey to identify the source of the Nile. T tells of Stanley's departure and Livingstone's death.

Paragraph 3 (STUQR)

The given sentence introduces the sport of Cricket. S defines the premise of the game and T follows to explain that different variations that can be found throughout England. U then describes the rise in popularity of the game which leads into Q. Q discusses the formation of the Code of 1744 which provided consistency of rules. R concludes by discussing the continued evolution of the game and its worldwide popularity.

Paragraph 4 (QRTSU)

The topic sentence introduces the battles that were fought in the sky during World War I. Q follows by identifying its participants as fighter pilots, and explaining that most fighter pilots only ever achieved a few victories before dying themselves. R then introduces the Red Baron as an exception who achieved several victories throughout his career as a fighter pilot. T follows with the Red Baron's real name as Manfred von Richthofen. S must follow because it's the only other sentence that refers to him as Richthofen. U ends the paragraph with the Red Baron's death after his 80th kill.

Paragraph 5 (RUSQT)

The given sentence gives Louis Braille's place and date of birth. R follows to describe how he became blind at the age of three. U follows to state that he attended the Royal Institute for the blind as a young man. S introduces the technique of "night writing" which leads to how in Q Louis adapted the soldier's code and used it to create a written language for the blind. T is last as it gives the term for tor the writing system, Braille, discussed in Q.

——— TEST FOURTEEN

PARAGRAPH 1

The roar of a tiger has the power to temporarily paralyze anything within earshot.

_____ **Q.** Infrasound refers to sound that is lower than 20 hertz, a frequency that is out of the human range of hearing.

_____ **R.** Therefore, when the tiger roars, frequencies this low are most likely produced.

_____ **S.** Scientists have yet to discover how the tiger achieves this, but they now think it may involve the use of infrasound.

_____ **T.** Researchers recently studied and recorded every sound a group of 24 Tigers can make and found that they often communicate below 18 hertz.

_____ **U.** Given these findings, scientists now hypothesize that the paralysis is caused by the loudness of the sound combined with the low frequencies.

PARAGRAPH 2

In order to understand how and why pearls are formed by fresh water oysters, we must first understand how oysters are constructed.

_____ **Q.** The resulting pearls have been prized for thousands of years.

_____ **R.** A material called nacre lines the inside of these shells and keeps them together as they grow.

_____ **S.** Oysters are bivalves, meaning they have shells made of two separate parts.

_____ **T.** If a foreign substance gets stuck inside its shell, a pearl will cover up the irritant with the nacre, which in time forms a pearl.

_____ **U.** An organ called the mantle is responsible for producing these shells and enabling their growth.

PARAGRAPH 3

The Taj Mahal of India is considered one of the most impressive buildings ever built.

_____ **Q.** It was constructed because Emperor Shah Jehan wanted to build a mausoleum for his wife, Mumtaz Mahal.

_____ **R.** Ustad's design combined the best of Persian, Central Asian, and Islamic architecture.

_____ **S.** The finished Taj Mahal took 22 years to complete, and was built by over 20,000 workers and costs thirty-two million rupees.

_____ **T.** Hundreds of designs were brought before him, and after choosing the design from architect Ustad Isa, Jehan gave orders for the construction to commence.

_____ **U.** This beautiful monument draws over two million visitors every year and has the honor of being listed as one of the Wonders of the Ancient World.

PARAGRAPH 4

Frisbee golf, also known as "disk golf", is a competitive and organized form of the traditional game of Frisbee; the goal of this game is to hit key targets in the fewest throws.

_____ **Q.** As the game became more popular, signs and hydrants made way for simpler, "standard" targets.

_____ **R.** Three types of Frisbees are used to score points, and the players' distance from these targets dictates which frisbee is employed.

_____ **S.** The sport of Frisbee golf continues to grow in popularity, with official courses popping up all over the United States.

_____ **T.** The game was invented by George Sappenfield of California, and was traditionally played using already established objects such as street signs and fire hydrants.

_____ **U.** The standard targets are uniform in size with baskets attached, and the courses typically have 18 holes.

PARAGRAPH 5

The North Star has been an invaluable guide to walking travelers and mariners for several centuries.

_____ **Q.** If you can locate this fixed star, you will be able to get yourself back on course, wherever you are.

_____ **R.** Its name derives from its North Pole location, which also gives it the name "Pole Star."

_____ **S.** While other stars gradually move during the night, the Pole Star remains in a fixed position just above polar north.

_____ **T.** For example, if you are in the Northern Hemisphere, you just need to look due north in order to find it.

_____ **U.** For a final tip, the North Star is always located halfway between Cassiopeia and the Big Dipper.

ANSWERS & EXPLANATIONS: TEST FOURTEEN

Paragraph 1 (SQTRU)

The given sentence describes the paralyzing power of a tiger's roar. S is next, stating that infrasound might be the cause of this paralysis. Q continues with a definition of Infrasound. T then goes on to describe the recent research done with tigers and the measurement of their various sounds. R explains that the low frequency of these sounds corresponds with the infrasound definition. U concludes with the hypothesis that resulted from these findings.

Paragraph 2 (SURTQ)

The topic sentence introduces pearls and their formation. The next three sentences describe the makeup of oysters. S explains that oysters are bivalves meaning they have shells made of two separate parts. U follows to describe the mantle which produces the shell. R then defines nacre as the lining inside of the shell. T explains how pearls are formed from these oysters. Q concludes the paragraph stating the great worth of the resulting pearls.

Paragraph 3 (QTRSU)

The given sentence introduces the Taj Mahal of India as one of the most impressive structures ever built. Q follows to describe the purpose of the monument as well as the Emperors requirements for it. T is next, naming Ustad Isa as the architect whose design was chosen for the Taj Mahal out of hundreds of others. R describes all the architectural influences that Ustad implemented in his design. S is next listing the years, manpower, and amount of money it took to complete the monument. U concludes the paragraph stating that the Taj Mahal is listed as one of the Wonders of the Ancient World.

Paragraph 4 (TQURS)

The given sentence introduces the sport of Frisbee Golf. T names the inventor of the game and explains how it was originally played using established targets like fire hydrants and street signs. Q follows explaining that as it became more popular, "standard targets" were introduced. U elaborates on the design of these standard targets. R mentions the three different Frisbees used to score points off the targets. S concludes the paragraph stating that Frisbee Golf continues to grow in popularity.

Paragraph 5 (RSQTU)

The given sentence introduces the North Star and its use in guiding travelers. R provides the star's alternate name, Pole Star, and attributes the name to its location. S then gives "the Pole Star's" location as fixed above polar north. Q explains why it is important to know how to locate it. T provides an example in support of Q, followed by U giving "a final tip" regarding the North Star's location.

—— TEST FIFTEEN

PARAGRAPH 1

Diamonds have long been considered a symbol of wealth and status, yet few are aware of the origins of these fine gemstones.

_____ **Q.** The diamonds are contained in these pieces, and are usually found in sedimentary deposits along coastlines and trenches.

_____ **R.** These areas are called, "diamond stability zones' and are conducive to the extremely high temperatures and pressure necessary for the formation of these gemstones.

_____ **S.** The diamonds are then brought to the surface through volcanic eruptions.

_____ **T.** These eruptions bring pieces of the mantle to the surface of the earth.

_____ **U.** For example, commercial diamonds, the diamonds we use for jewelry, are formed in the earth's mantle underneath continental plates.

PARAGRAPH 2

The La Brea Tar Pits of California provide a window into the animals that roamed the earth millions of years ago.

_____ **Q.** Layer upon layer of sediment seeped out of the ground over the centuries and preserved the trapped animals.

_____ **R.** Tar pits are large pools of crude oil which form along the earth's surface, and despite their name, they contain no tar at all.

_____ **S.** Nearly three million of these fossils have been preserved in the La Brea Tar Pits for over 40,000 years.

_____ **T.** In an effort to attack these ensnared animals, predators will often find themselves stuck as well.

_____ **U.** Asphalt seeps into low lying areas and are soft and sticky, trapping animals who attempt to pass through them.

PARAGRAPH 3

Stradivarius violins were crafted In Cremona, Italy by Antonio Stradivari in the 18th century.

_____ **Q.** They are now owned by private collectors or safeguarded in the world's finest museums.

_____ **R.** Their high value is attributed to their purity of sound and unique structure.

_____ **S.** Stradivarius' are prized for their sound, versatility, and power.

_____ **T.** Stradivari is thought to have made over 1,000 violins during his life-time; 650 of those have survived over the centuries.

_____ **U.** These surviving violins are prized by musicians, and sell for millions of dollars.

PARAGRAPH 4

Chalk Airlines is the world's first scheduled airline and was founded by Arthur Burns "Pappy" Chalk in 1919.

_____ **Q.** Chalk sold his company in 1966 and the airline is still in service today.

_____ **R.** In the 1930's, the airline mainly traveled between the United States and the Bahamas.

_____ **S.** Later during WWII, Chalk few submarine patrols around southern Florida to assure the U.S. coasts were safe.

_____ **T.** He began with a single Stinson Voyager seaplane and charged $5 for sightseeing, and $15 for flying lessons.

_____ **U.** During prohibition in the 1920's, Al Capone and other gangsters used Chalk airlines to travel around.

PARAGRAPH 5

The Shepherd Clock of England has been keeping time for the world since 1852.

_____ **Q.** As for the dial, it had already been in use since the 13th century.

_____ **R.** The clock is located outside of the Royal Observatory and displays Greenwich Mean Time to the second by using a 24-hour dial.

_____ **S.** Moreover, it is controlled by electronic pulses sent by a master clock located in the observatory.

_____ **T.** These pulses were initially sent around the country by electric telegraph exchange and traveled across the ocean via transatlantic cable.

_____ **U.** However, the clock's current dial is not the original as the first dial was destroyed by a bomb during WWII.

ANSWERS & EXPLANATIONS: TEST FIFTEEN

Paragraph 1 (URSTQ)

The topic sentence states that diamonds can be formed by one of four major processes. U follows explaining that the diamonds used for jewelry are formed deep within the earth's mantle. R must follow as it gives the name of the area where the diamonds are formed. S then describes how these diamonds are brought to the surface. T is next stating that the eruptions discussed in S bring pieces of mantel to the surface. Q concludes explaining that the diamonds are contained in the pieces of mantel referred to in T.

Paragraph 2 (RUTQS)

The given sentence introduces the La Brea Tar Pits. R follows explaining they are not actually made of tar. U defines the structure of the tar pit, explaining that these asphalt seeps pooled in low lying areas and are known to trap passing animals. T describes how the predators then became stuck when they attacked the animals mentioned in U. Q then explains how the layers of sediment preserved their bones. S concludes and states that three million of these fossils have been reserved.

Paragraph 3 (TUSRQ)

The given sentence introduces the maker and origin of the Stradivarius violins. T leads with, "He is thought to have made close to 1,000 violins..." (With *he referring back to Antonio Stradivari in the given sentence.)* It then states how many violins survived the years. U connects to T with, "These surviving violins..." and then states that they are prized by musicians. S and R follow to describe why they are prized. S must come first as indicated by its lead, "They are prized..." which connects back to T. R then follows with a description of their sound. Q concludes by stating where the remaining Stradivarius' are currently located.

Paragraph 4 (TURSQ)

The given sentence introduces Chalk airlines as the world's first scheduled airline. T explains how the company began. The next three sentences follow in order of date. With U (1920's) followed by R (1930's) and then S (1940's). Q concludes the paragraph stating that the airline is still in service today.

Paragraph 5 (RSTQU)

The given sentence introduces the Shepherd Clock of England and its purpose. R follows to give its exact location. S then explains how the clock works followed by T which explains how the pulses mentioned in T were transmitted. Q states that the design of the dial has been used since the 13th Century. U then explains that the current dial is not the original.

—— TEST SIXTEEN

PARAGRAPH 1

Florida is built on thick carbonate deposits which are easily eroded by the circulating ground water.

_____ **Q.** The sinkhole dilemma could be controlled by addressing Florida's overpopulation which causes heavy ground-water pumping and over surface loading.

_____ **R.** Sinkholes are depressions in the land that will eventually collapse.

_____ **S.** One environmental concern is that sinkholes can drain into streams and wetlands depositing harmful chemicals into Florida's water supply.

_____ **T.** When a sinkhole opens up, it can cause significant damage not only to property but also to the environment.

_____ **U.** This erosion has resulted in an increase in sinkholes which cause millions of dollars in damage every year.

PARAGRAPH 2

When sailors refer to high tide versus low tide, they are technically speaking about the vertical movement of the water.

_____ **Q.** These high and low tides occur approximately six hours apart.

_____ **R.** Nevertheless, it is vital that one is able to make these predictions, especially if one is approaching a potentially shallow port or harbor.

_____ **S.** In addition, the tidal cycle will repeat itself approximately fifty minutes later than the day before, making tides fairly predictable.

_____ **T.** The moon's gravitational pull causes the tidal cycle to consist of two high tides and two low tides each day.

_____ **U.** Believe it or not, these tides are actually affected by the moon.

PARAGRAPH 3

Stonehenge is a site located in Wiltshire, England and was built towards the end of the "New Stone Age".

_____ **Q.** Many speculate about the purpose of Stonehenge and how it came about.

_____ **R.** Arthurian legend suggests they were brought from Ireland under the orders of Merlin.

_____ **S.** The giant stones that make up Stonehenge are known as megaliths that are arranged inside a circle and into a horseshoe shape.

_____ **T.** The name Stonehenge derives from "Stone Hinge," which means Giant Stone.

_____ **U.** Whatever its origins, Stonehenge stands in the 21st Century as the most significant prehistoric monument in all of Britain.

PARAGRAPH 4

Census of Marine Life researchers from over 80 nations took part in a ten year study of ocean life.

_____ **Q.** To record diversity, Census researchers formed a global list of all forms of sea life, adding more than 5,600 new species to the list of identified marine life.

_____ **R.** This ambitious study will help scientists protect our living oceans for years to come.

_____ **S.** Meanwhile, the research on animal distribution mapped each animal's territory and is used to monitor the effects of global change on marine populations.

_____ **T.** Finally, these researchers tracked the abundance of each marine creature by estimating how many of these species reside in our oceans.

_____ **U.** The purpose of this study was to catalogue the diversity, distribution, and abundance of all marine life.

PARAGRAPH 5

Ralph Bunche was a Diplomat known for his ability to negotiate between enemy nations.

_____ **Q.** While working for the U.N., he negotiated the 1949 Armistice between Israel and the surrounding Arab nations.

_____ **R.** After college, Bunche worked as a professor and then joined the State Department until finally joining the United Nations.

_____ **S.** Bunche received the Nobel Peace Prize for his work and soon became Undersecretary General of the U.N. where he continued to promote peace for the remainder of his career.

_____ **T.** He then continued his education, going on to become the first African American to earn a Ph.D. from Harvard's government department.

_____ **U.** Long before then, the orphaned Bunche attended the University of Central Los Angeles on a full athletic scholarship.

ANSWERS & EXPLANATIONS: TEST SIXTEEN

Paragraph 1 (URTSQ)

The topic sentence explains the problem with Florida's foundation. U then states that this problem causes sinkholes. R defines these sinkholes explaining that they are depressions in the land which will eventually collapse. T then describes the damage caused to property by the collapsed sinkholes. S follows by providing an example of environmental damage, which was introduced in T. Q concludes by introducing one cause, and with that, a possible solution.

Paragraph 2 (UTQSR)

The given sentence introduces the high and low tide distinction while defining "tide" itself. U states that this distinction is actually determined by the moon. T explains this further by discussing the moon's gravitational pull, which causes the tidal cycle. Q states that these high and low tides occur approximately six hours apart. S states that tides occur fifty minutes later than the prior day, but R stresses that although one can predict tides, boaters should still be aware of sudden changes.

Paragraph 3 (TSQRU)

The topic sentence gives the location of Stonehenge. T defines the meaning of Stonehenge and states it is named for its enormous standing stones. S follows with the technical name of these stones and how they were constructed. Q introduces the mystery as to their original use and creation. R introduces the origin story from the Arthurian legend. U concludes with a statement of their significance to Britain.

Paragraph 4 (UQSTR)

The given sentence introduces the Census of Marine Life's 10 year study. U then follows to give the purpose of this study: diversity, distribution, and abundance. The next three sentences describe each of those purposes in the order presented in sentence U with Q defining diversity, S defining distribution, and T defining abundance. R then concludes by describing how this study will positively impact our oceans.

Paragraph 5 (UTRQS)

The given sentence introduces Ralph Bunche and his ability to achieve the seemingly impossible. The remaining paragraph describes his major achievements. U discusses Bunche's childhood continuing through his admission into college. T then begins with, "He then continued his education…" The next three sentences discuss Bunche's career. R links to T with, "after college," and states that Bunche began to work for the United Nations. Q then starts with. "It was while working for the U.N…" and tells about the armistice he negotiated. S wraps up this paragraph with Bunche's award of the Nobel Peace Prize for the armistice he negotiated in Q.

—— TEST SEVENTEEN

PARAGRAPH 1

The well-preserved cliff dwellings of North America's Mesa Verde date back to the 1190s.

_____ **Q.** It is estimated that between twenty five thousand and fifty thousand Pueblo inhabited these homes.

_____ **R.** The native Pueblo built their homes underneath the cliffs and farmed the tops of the mesa for nearly a century.

_____ **S.** Nearly 600 of these cliff dwellings are still intact.

_____ **T.** The smallest cliff dwellings made up just one room while the largest contained more than 150 rooms.

_____ **U.** By 1300, the Pueblo left the cliffs abandoned, and migrated to the land that is now known as New Mexico and Arizona.

PARAGRAPH 2

Caves are like cavities located underground in the earth's crust.

_____ **Q.** When this water builds up, it forms rock stalagmites along the ground as well as stalactites on the ceiling.

_____ **R.** The stalagmites and stalactites we see in caves today were centuries in the making, taking over 100 years to grow a mere inch.

_____ **S.** This water slowly dissolves the rock along cracks and passages as chambers gradually form over the millenniums.

_____ **T.** Most of them are formed due to the dissolving action of slightly acidic underground water.

_____ **U.** This is why caves often contain interconnected passages and levels within their walls.

PARAGRAPH 3

Indira Gandhi served as Prime Minister of India from 1966-1977 and again from 1980 – 1984.

_____ **Q.** Her father became the first Prime Minister of India after it was granted independence from Britain.

_____ **R.** Although Gandhi demonstrated strong leadership skills, many felt she was too authoritative and failed to make the changes she had promised.

_____ **S.** Moreover, Gandhi became the first woman ever to be elected to lead a democracy.

_____ **T.** She was a member of the Working Committee and won her position by promising to rid her nation of poverty.

_____ **U.** Tragically, Indira Gandhi was assassinated by her bodyguards and her son Rahiv succeeded her as Prime Minister.

PARAGRAPH 4

Water is one of our most precious resources, but while three fourths of our world is covered in water, only three percent of the earth's water is potable.

_____ **Q.** Of that three percent, all but one percent is underground, frozen in icecaps and glaciers.

_____ **R.** Therefore we must find alternative methods of creating drinkable water; perhaps the best method is by using "reverse osmosis," but this process is far too expensive to be a viable option at this time.

_____ **S.** Currently, scientists are creating new ways of desalinating salt water to meet the needs of our growing world population.

_____ **T.** This process of desalination turns saltwater into fresh, drinking water.

_____ **U.** Because desalination is extremely expensive, scientists are studying new methods for cutting down the costs of purifying water.

PARAGRAPH 5

Pumpkins come in many varieties and can range anywhere from a few ounces to over five hundred pounds.

_____ **Q.** Once the pumpkins begin to grow, make sure to place something under them to prevent them from rotting.

_____ **R.** After choosing a fit location for size and sunlight, bury five seeds in a circular fashion beneath the dirt.

_____ **S.** In order to plant pumpkins, seeds should be placed in a location where they will receive a minimum of six hours of direct sunlight every day.

_____ **T.** While planting the seeds, make sure they are completely covered so they are not eaten by birds.

_____ **U.** Pumpkins also need plenty of room to grow because they often sprout vines and can become quite large.

ANSWERS & EXPLANATIONS: TEST SEVENTEEN

Paragraph 1 (RQSTU)

The given sentence introduces the cliff dwellings of Mesa Verde stating that they are the best preserved in North America. S supports this idea by stating that there are 600 cliff dwellings still intact. R describes where these homes were built. T describes how they were structured. Q is next stating that there were between 25,000 and 50,000 pueblos inhabiting the homes described in R and T at their peak. U concludes with the migration of the Pueblo and the abandonment of the cliff homes.

Paragraph 2 (TSUQR)

The topic sentence defines caves. T then begins the explanation of how they are formed. S continues by explaining that the process takes thousands of years. U describes what the final structure looks like. Q then describes the effect of water deposits. R concludes with a statement on how long these deposits take to develop into stalagmites and stalactites.

Paragraph 3 (QTSRU)

The given sentence introduces Indira Gandhi as the Prime Minister of India for fifteen years. Q gives her political background and T follows giving the name of her party and the platform on which she won the election. S states that she was the first woman ever elected to lead a democracy. R continues explaining that, although she was a strong leader, many felt she was too authoritative and failed to live up to her promises. U concludes with her assassination in 1984.

Paragraph 4 (QSTRU)

The given sentence states that water is our most precious resource and then gives the percentage of fresh water available. Q continues explaining that of that fresh water only one percent is usable. S then explains that scientist have found ways to desalinate salt water to meet the needs of our growing world population. T is next and defines desalination. R then follows explaining that the cost of desalination is still very high. U is last and states that scientists are trying to find ways to reduce the costs associated with it.

Paragraph 5 (SURTQ)

The given sentence explains that pumpkins come in an array of varieties and sizes. S states that when choosing a spot to grow pumpkins, it is important that they receive a minimum of six hours of direct sunlight every day. U then explains that pumpkins also need plenty of room to grow. R follows leading with, "Once you have chosen your spot..." and goes on to describe how they are to be planted. T then explains pumpkins must be completely covered or they will be eaten by birds. Q concludes by explaining that once the pumpkins begin to grow something must be placed under them to prevent rotting.

—— TEST EIGHTEEN

PARAGRAPH 1

Harriet Chalmers Adams was a world class adventurer and geographer.

_____ Q. During her childhood, Adams learned how to horseback ride, hunt, and fish.

_____ R. Adams was denied membership status in the National Geographic Society, which led her to found the Society of Women Geographers.

_____ S. By the time of her death, Adams had canoed down the Amazon, traveled across Europe, and successfully discovered over 20 unchartered territories.

_____ T. After marrying her husband, Franklin Pierce Adams, the two traveled through South America visiting every country on its continent.

_____ U. During these three years of travel, she wrote articles and provided her pictures to National Geographic Magazine.

PARAGRAPH 2

Helicopters have the unique ability to access three dimensional space.

_____ Q. This cyclic stick changes the pitch of one blade at a time, which enables the helicopter to navigate all possible directions in the sky.

_____ R. The direction is then controlled by a cyclic stick controlled by the pilot.

_____ S. Once the larger blade begins to rotate, it forces a large amount of air downward to create the lift.

_____ T. Their ingenious design includes two pairs of propellers, the larger of which is located above its cab with the smaller one on the tip of its tail.

_____ U. This larger blade helps the helicopter fly while the smaller one keeps the vessel stable to prevent spinning.

PARAGRAPH 3

Antlion larvae set an elaborate trap in the form of a conical pit in order to catch their prey.

_____ **Q.** When its prey's movement alerts the antlion, they leap out from the bottom of the pit and capture insects with their enormous jaws.

_____ **R.** This unusual creature digs this pit by using its jaws to release sand as it circles the hole.

_____ **S.** The larvae will then lie in waiting for their prey to fall into this trap.

_____ **T.** Once it has achieved the appropriate depth and slope, the antillon will bury itself just beneath the surface of the pit.

_____ **U.** Alas, the pit's steep walls make it nearly impossible for the insect to escape, as the soft sand provides no traction.

PARAGRAPH 4

Rising populations have led to more cars than ever on the roads, resulting in more traffic congestion in big cities throughout the world.

_____ **Q.** One possible solution for tracking traffic is the Cellocate system.

_____ **R.** The computer then uses triangulation to identify the driver's position on the highway and sends personalized traffic warnings to the drivers.

_____ **S.** It is estimated that, in the United States, almost 7 billion gallons of fuel were wasted last year while drivers sat in traffic jams alone.

_____ **T.** This system collects, decodes, and time-stamps cell phone transmissions gathered together from listening posts and sends all the data to a centralized computer.

_____ **U.** Thankfully, government transportation agencies are looking towards technological solutions to alleviate the problems caused by congestion and fuel waste.

PARAGRAPH 5

Draw bridges are used to allow ships to navigate waterways when they are too tall to sail underneath the bridge.

_____ Q. While each structure is designed specifically for their intended location, they are all made of concrete and steel.

_____ R. The double leaf bridge is the most common draw bridge design; it opens in the middle and lifts on both sides.

_____ S. Each leaf is counterbalanced with a weight on the opposite side of the pivot axle which descends as the bridge opens.

_____ T. They were originally called "bascule bridges" in France which means seesaw.

_____ U. Newer draw bridges are being constructed to be lighter and more efficient than those currently in use.

ANSWERS & EXPLANATIONS: TEST EIGHTEEN

Paragraph 1 (QTURS)

The given sentence introduces Harriet Chalmers Adams and the time period in which she lived. Q describes her childhood providing the background for her later life as an adventurer. T is next introducing her marriage and subsequent journey to South America. U states that during this time she provided articles and pictures to National Geographic. Next is R explaining that she was not allowed membership to the society because she was a woman, which inspired her to create a woman's geographic society. S concludes the paragraph listing all of Adams' major accomplishments as an adventurer.

Paragraph 2 (TUSRQ)

The given sentence describes the unique ability of helicopters to access three dimensional space. The remainder of the paragraph explains how this process works. T introduces the two propellers with U then stating the purpose of each. S follows, describing how the helicopter achieves lift. R then describes how it achieves movement in various directions. Q concludes the sentence referencing the specific ways the cyclic stick allows the helicopter to move to achieve the three dimensional space referred to in the topic sentence.

Paragraph 3 (RTSUQ)

The given sentence describes the trap an antlion sets to catch its prey. R follows to explain how the antlion digs this trap. T then explains that upon completion of the trap the antlion buries itself in the bottom of the pit. S then states that it lies in waiting there until its prey stumbles in. U explains why it is nearly impossible for the insect to escape once it has fallen into the trap. Q concludes the paragraph with the antlion catching and consuming the insect.

Paragraph 4 (SUQTR)

The given sentence introduces the problem of increase congestion on the roadways in big cities. S gives an estimate of the amount of fuel wasted due to this congestion. U follows explaining that government transportation agencies are looking to technology to alleviate this problem. The next three sentences describe one possible solution. Q introduces the Cellocate system which is being used in some test areas to track traffic. T follows to describe how this system works. R concludes the sentence by describing how the system then uses triangulation to send personalized traffic warnings to the drivers.

Paragraph 5 (TRSQU)

The given sentence describes the use of drawbridges. Sentence T gives the original name for draw bridges. The next three sentences describe the mechanics of the bridge. R describes the way they open for ship traffic. S then explains how the leaves are counterbalanced. Q follows stating that all draw bridges are made of concrete and steel. U concludes by discussing the structure of current models of draw bridges.

—— TEST NINETEEN

PARAGRAPH 1

Hovercrafts are multipurpose vehicles that allow the driver to navigate on water, ice, land, or snow.

_____ Q. As this process can work anywhere there is air, hovercrafts have been used for a multitude of purposes, most notably as a military transport, to deliver mail, and even as ferry to transport people and cars.

_____ R. Each has a propeller which sits atop the rear of the craft and powers the engine.

_____ S. In addition, an impeller acts as a powerful fan which forces the surrounding air down below the vehicle.

_____ T. This allows the craft to push this air out the back which then forces the hovercraft to go forward.

_____ U. The hovercraft is also bordered by a skirt, which corrals this pressurized air underneath the craft.

PARAGRAPH 2

Lipizzaner stallions were named for Lipica, a small village in Slovenia where they were first bred during the 16th century in order to create light, fast horses.

_____ Q. These purebred horses are average sized horses with black coats that go grey as they age.

_____ R. Throughout their life, these stallions compete and often win prizes for their high-stepping gait and their perfect dressage abilities.

_____ S. Luckily, these unique horses evaded extinction during World War II when General Patton smuggled them out from behind enemy lines declaring them to be, "More precious than jewels."

_____ T. Originally bred only for the Austrian-Hungarian monarchy, Lipizzaner stallions remain a rare breed even today.

_____ **U.** Moreover, there are less than 3,000 purebred Lipizzans in the world representing over 400 years of breeding from six original stallion lines.

PARAGRAPH 3

Blast-resistant suits are most often used by law enforcement officers and military personnel.

_____ **Q.** Their purpose is to provide protection from the dangers associated with explosives.

_____ **R.** To protect against the shrapnel the front and back have ballistic plates made from Kevlar and positioned on top of these fibers.

_____ **S.** Finally, the entire suit is flame-resistant in order to neutralize heat and flames from a blast.

_____ **T.** The fibers in a blast resistant suit are woven extremely tightly in order to spread impact out over the surface of the suit.

_____ **U.** These dangers include impact foce, flying debris, and fire.

PARAGRAPH 4

The Porcelain Tower of Nanjing once overlooked the Yangtze River in Nanjing, China

_____ **Q.** Sadly, this great tower was destroyed during the Taiping Revolution when it was vandalized and eventually destroyed.

_____ **R.** Its design was just as impressive as its height, featuring white porcelain bricks decorated with glazes and stoneware as well as images of animals, flowers, and landscapes.

_____ **S.** These nine stories equated to 260 feet, making it one of the tallest buildings in China.

_____ **T.** At this time, the tower was nine stories high and had an octagonal base topped with a golden sphere.

_____ **U.** It was originally constructed as a Buddhist place of worship during the 15th century.

PARAGRAPH 5

Akbar the Great's reign as ruler of the Indian empire began in 1556 at the age of thirteen.

_____ **Q.** In addition, Akbar was a great patron of the arts, spawning a Renaissance within music and literature right alongside the kingdom's political expansion.

_____ **R.** It is no wonder that historians have hailed Akbar as the greatest ruler of Indian history, further dubbing him, "the glory of the Indian empire."

_____ **S.** During his half-century reign, Akbar extended the Indian borders from Afghanistan to the East all the way to the Godavari River to the West.

_____ **T.** He also supported the distinctive Mughal architectural style, which can be seen all throughout the royal city, Fatepur Sikri.

_____ **U.** Fatepur Sikri prominently reflects this architectural approach with its shapely domes, minarets, and delicate ornamentation.

ANSWERS & EXPLANATIONS: TEST NINETEEN

Paragraph 1 (RSUTQ)

The given sentence introduces hovercrafts as multipurpose vehicles that can travel over any terrain. The next four sentences describe how hovercrafts work. R explains that the propeller powers the engine. S leads with, "They also have an impeller…" and describes how it forces air below the vehicle. U is next and explains how the hovercrafts skirt corrals the air collected in S. T then explains how the air corralled in U is pushed out the back forcing the hovercraft forward. Q concludes the paragraph listing the various purposes hovercrafts.

Paragraph 2 (TUQRS)

The topic sentence introduces the history behind the name of the Lipizzaner stallion and the purpose behind its breeding. T follows stating that they were originally bred only for the monarchy and that they are still a rare breed today. U supports this statement by stating there are only 3,000 of these horses in the world. Q follows to describe the physical characteristics of the breed followed by R describing the qualities that make them a prized creature. S concludes the paragraph explaining how Lipizzaners were saved from near extinction and declared to be, "More precious than jewels."

Paragraph 3 (QUTRS)

The given sentence explains which occupations utilize blast-resistant suits. Q gives the purpose of a blast resistant suit which is to protect the wearer from danger associated with a blast. U follows and lists the three major dangers associated with a blast. The next three sentences explain how its design protects against each of the dangers listed in U in the same order they were listed. T describes how the blast suit's fibers are woven in such a way, as to spread the blast out over the surface of the suit. R goes on to explain how the garments Kevlar creates protect the wearer form shrapnel. S concludes the paragraph with an explanation of the suit's flame-resistant material.

Paragraph 4 (UTSRQ)

The given sentence introduces the Porcelain Tower of Nanjing. Sentence U explains when and why it was originally built. T is next and describes what the tower looks like. S then states it was one of the tallest buildings in China at the time of its construction. R follows leading with, "Its decorations were as impressive as its architecture…" and goes on to further describe these decorations. Q then concludes the paragraph with the tower's destruction during the Taiping Revolution.

Paragraph 5 (STUQR)

The given sentence states that Akbar the Great began his reign of India at the age of thirteen. S follows describing the length of his reign and the growth of India's territory during this time. T then states that Akbar appreciated the Mughal architectural style and used the style throughout India's newly acquired territories, specifically in the construction of the royal city of Fatepur Sikri. U follows to explain the specific architectural aspects of this style (minarets, domes, and ornamentation). Q is next stating that music and literature experienced a renaissance alongside the growth of the kingdom. This suggests that it must come after T and U rather than before these choices. R concludes the paragraph with the statement that Akbar is thought to have been the greatest ruler in Indian history.

———TEST TWENTY

PARAGRAPH 1

Ivan IV, better known as Ivan the Terrible, became the first Czar of Russia on January 16, 1547.

_____ **Q.** The name "Terrible" was given to him by his people, and is best translated to mean formidable or awesome.

_____ **R.** He also opened up trade and created a standing army to protect the country and his people.

_____ **S.** Unfortunately, the last part of Ivan's reign was marked by war, and Russia was left destitute and in ruins at the time of his death.

_____ **T.** One of his first initiatives was to modernize Russia and update many of the country's laws.

_____ **U.** He became a Czar at the young age 16 and did much to improve Russia during the first half of his reign.

PARAGRAPH 2

The naked mole rat is a hairless, burrowing rodent native to East Africa.

_____ **Q.** In order to prevent dirt from filling their mouth while they eat, the naked mole rat's lips form a seal behind their teeth.

_____ **R.** Much like ants and bees, naked mole rats organize themselves into colonies with specific job functions for each member of the group.

_____ **S.** They are less than three inches tall, and although their legs are tiny, these sand puppies can burrow underground with their teeth.

_____ **T.** This structure is one of the reasons they have the longest lifespan of any other rodent, living well over 20 years.

_____ **U.** Also called sand puppies, these strange creatures are well designed for their life underground.

PARAGRAPH 3

Archeological discoveries have shown that libraries have existed nearly as long as the written word.

_____ **Q.** At its peak, this library once held nearly over 750,000 scrolls until fires during the Roman occupation destroyed the library and all its contents.

_____ **R.** But the most famous ancient library was the Great Library of Alexandria, founded by Egypt's King Ptolemy around 300 B.C.

_____ **S.** Ptolemy's goal was to create a universal library that would contain a half-million scrolls for the public use.

_____ **T.** Thus, he collected works from all over the known world, which were rolled and stored into pigeon holds with their name written on a wooden label and hung from the end of each scroll.

_____ **U.** Ancient Mesopotamian clay tablets are the first evidence we have of early libraries.

PARAGRAPH 4

The Mayan civilization occupied the Yucatan Peninsula of Mexico for six centuries

_____ **Q.** In addition, the Mayans were fascinated by astronomy and they built several observatories to study the night sky.

_____ **R.** Along with these observatories, the Mayans built great pyramids that ascend above the jungle canopy and were used primarily for religious observances.

_____ **S.** They were an advanced society and had a written language as well as a detailed calendar.

_____ **T.** Mayan society continued to thrive until their cities were all mysteriously abandoned between 300 and 900 AD.

_____ **U.** But the Mayans didn't only work; they were also sports enthusiasts and they built ball courts primarily for a game called pitz.

PARAGRAPH 5

Wind power is a renewable form of energy that is better for the environment than today's popular fossil fuels.

_____ Q.   With the current focus on conservation and non-sustainable fossil fuels, wind energy is quickly becoming a viable alternative energy option.

_____ R.   Sailors in Ancient Egypt first harvested wind energy as they used wind to propel their sailboats.

_____ S.   Windmills would later be used in Europe when Crusaders brought the idea back from the Middle East.

_____ T.   Wind energy was first used to supply electricity to rural areas during the 1930's.

_____ U.   This practice continued in the Middle East, when Babylonians used windmills to grind grain.

ANSWERS & EXPLANATIONS: TEST TWENTY

Paragraph 1 (QUTRS)

The topic sentence introduces Ivan IV of Russia. Q explains the reason for his famous name. U gives the age at which Ivan became Czar and states that he did much to improve Russia during the first half of his reign. T then leads with, "One of his first initiatives…" and therefore continues to describe his rein. R further explicates these initiatives in more detail. S follows by citing the final stage of his reign leading up to his death.

Paragraph 2 (USQRT)

The given sentence introduces the naked mole rat. U follows giving their other name (sand puppy) and states that they are well designed for life underground. S is next as it describes the characteristics referred to in U ending with their large teeth. Q follows to explain their ability to seal their lips behind their teeth to prevent their mouth from filling with dirt as they dig. R and T describe the colonies social structure with R comparing it to that of ants and bees .T then concludes the paragraph stating that this structure contributes to their long lifespan.

Paragraph 3 (URSTQ)

The topic sentence states that libraries have been around for as long as the written word. U follows to support that statement with the description of clay tablets found in Ancient Mesopotamia over 5,000 years ago. R is next, introducing the most famous ancient library, *The Great Library of Alexandria.* S explains how it originated (King Ptolemy) and T then describes how the King collected its many works. Q concludes the paragraph with its destruction during the Roman occupation of Alexandria and the ensuing fires.

Paragraph 4 (SQRUT)

The given sentence introduces the Mayan civilization and its long rule on the Yucatan peninsula. S then goes on to describe them as an advanced society with the next three sentences giving examples. Q leads with their interest in Astronomy and states that they built observatories. R follows, leading with, "Besides observatories they also built…" going on to describe their pyramids. U then states that sports were also valued by the Mayans. T concludes with the mysterious abandonment of the major Mayan cities around 900 AD.

Paragraph 5 (RUSTQ)

The topic sentence states that scientists are looking to wind energy because it renewable. The remaining sentences describe the history of wind energy beginning with the Ancient Egyptians in R. U follows with the advent of the windmill and its spread throughout the Middle East. S then explains how windmills were established in Europe after the Crusaders brought the idea back from the Middle East. T then traces their later use in the United States before standard electricity was provided. Q concludes with a restating of the topic sentence.

INDEX

Made in the USA
Middletown, DE
08 October 2014